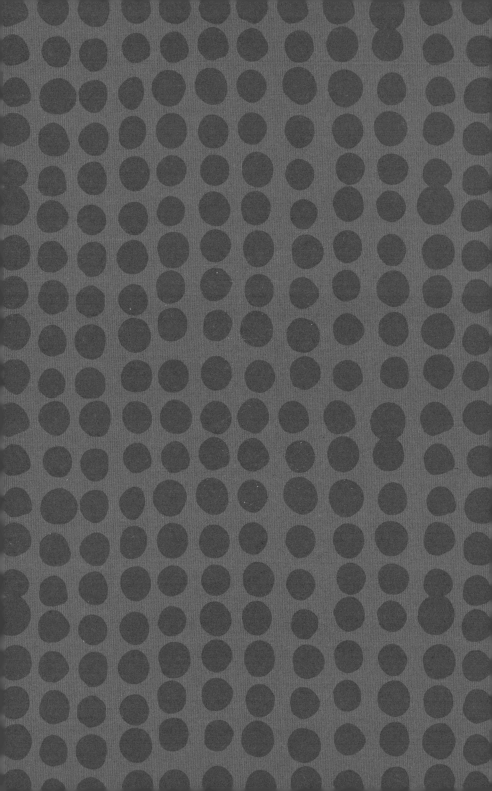

Praise for Jaime Schmidt and *Supermaker*

"Jaime Schmidt is the quintessential maker-made-good."

—*Inc.*

"Jaime's story of founding Schmidt's from her kitchen and growing it into a global brand is one for the ages."

—Paul Polman, former CEO of Unilever

"If you have an idea, follow Schmidt's playbook."

—*Forbes*

"[A] behind-the-scenes look at Schmidt's business strategies, designed to inspire and advise entrepreneurs hoping to follow a similar path to startup success."

—*Entrepreneur*

"If you don't already know and love Jaime Schmidt, you're about to."

—*Create & Cultivate*

SUPER MAKER

SUPER
MAKER

Crafting Business
on Your Own Terms

Jaime Schmidt

CHRONICLE PRISM

Library of Congress Cataloging-in-Publication Data

Names: Schmidt, Jaime, author.
Title: Supermaker : crafting business on your own terms / Jaime Schmidt.
Description: San Francisco, California : Chronicle Prism, [2020] | Summary: "Jaime Schmidt: acclaimed entrepreneur, founder of Schmidt's Naturals, and icon of the Maker Movement shares how you too can start or grow your own business with advice on branding, product development, social media marketing, scaling, PR, and customer engagement, all based on her own hard-won mastery"—Provided by publisher.
Identifiers: LCCN 2019056907 | ISBN 9781452184869 (hardcover) | ISBN 9781797201481 (ebook)
Subjects: LCSH: New business enterprises. | Small business—Growth.
Classification: LCC HD62.5 .S3525 2020 | DDC 658.1/1—dc23
LC record available at https://lccn.loc.gov/2019056907

Manufactured in the United States of America.

Design by Pamela Geismar.
Cover design, logo, illustrations, patterns, and dingbats by Rick DeLucco.
Typesetting by Maureen Forys, Happenstance Type-O-Rama.
Typeset in Montserrat and Tiempos Text.

10 9 8 7 6 5 4 3 2 1

Chronicle books and gifts are available at special quantity discounts to corporations, professional associations, literacy programs, and other organizations. For details and discount information, please contact our premiums department at corporatesales@chroniclebooks.com or at 1-800-759-0190.

CHRONICLE PRISM

Chronicle Prism is an imprint of Chronicle Books LLC, 680 Second Street, San Francisco, California 94107

www.chronicleprism.com

This book is dedicated to the creative community of makers and entrepreneurs everywhere who have provided endless inspiration.

Table of Contents

Part III **Make an Impact**

CHANGE THE LANDSCAPE + DISRUPT AN INDUSTRY

Part IV **Make It Last**

SUSTAIN YOUR PRODUCT + STAY TRUE TO YOUR PATH

Introduction

Every entrepreneur has a story. Each is passionate, driven, and committed to creating the best version of their product. Many have hopes of turning their passions into profit, and many are doing just that. But even for entrepreneurs with a groundbreaking product, perfectly curated Instagram feed, and connections to people of influence, it is excruciatingly difficult to advance to the next level. No matter the enterprise, anyone out there building their own business will encounter a landscape that is profoundly saturated, competitive, and fierce.

That's why each of these entrepreneurs is asking the same question: *How will I make it?*

Not long ago, I was one of them. I attended market upon market, carrying my supplies and faithful sidekick (my toddler, Oliver) in tow. I'd set up my folding table, drape a thrifted tablecloth over it, and arrange my lotions, sunscreens, soaps, and deodorants. Each item had been made by my hands in my kitchen, carefully poured into its respective Mason jar, and labeled with stickers my friend helped me create. I'd take a seat behind my modest products, look out at the sea of other makers, and on many long afternoons with few customers and little business, inevitably ask myself that very question: *How will I make it?*

I first joined the Maker Movement in 2010 in Portland, Oregon. At the time, it seemed everyone in the city was making and crafting. There was some comfort in that company, but it was also intimidating.

Within two years, I decided to focus entirely on my bestselling deodorant and stopped making other products. I moved production from my kitchen to my garage and then to a nearby warehouse. I couldn't keep up with the demand, so I hired two employees. My husband, Chris, helped me build a website, spurring orders from customers and retailers all over the world. We were suddenly a smash hit online, filling a niche for customers who had been seeking a natural deodorant that actually worked. Not long after, Chris left his job to run our marketing, which meant our family was fully invested in and dependent upon the success of Schmidt's Deodorant.

Before I knew it, Schmidt's was sold internationally and in big stores like Whole Foods and Urban Outfitters. A few years later, we were flying off the shelves at Target, Costco, and Walmart. The company grew into a multimillion-dollar brand with 150 employees and a presence in over thirty thousand retail accounts in thirty countries worldwide. Major consumer packaged goods (CPG) companies took note and wanted to buy my company. Seven years after starting the business, Schmidt's was acquired for nine figures by Unilever, the largest CPG company in the world, and I found myself with a deal securing both my family's financial future and the integrity of my product and creative vision.

I'd sold millions of units and earned millions of dollars—not for an app, device, or shiny new technology, but for deodorant, the stuff you put on your armpits each morning and hardly think about. Fueled by my own intuition, self-determination, and a natural recipe I had conceived of and believed in, I went from countless hours on my feet at the market to disrupting the landscape of an entire industry. The journey required not just an unrelenting faith in myself, but also a hard-won mastery of product development, customer support, branding, PR, digital marketing, and much more, including the ability to consistently innovate sooner and better than the competition.

The maker community gave me the courage to do what I love and the foundation upon which to forge my own path. But when I was in the throes of growing my business, I had to give it my complete attention, with hardly a moment to take a deep breath, let alone stay deeply connected to the community that had given me my start. Now that I have the time to step back and reflect on what helped me succeed, I've shifted my attention toward sharing the lessons I've learned and giving back to the community that launched my career.

Nowadays, the landscape is more congested and competitive than ever. Even innovative, purpose-driven brands that kick ass on social media must go the extra mile to stand out against others like them, offering specialized products that meet the needs of conscientious, sophisticated audiences. Facing increasing demands for authenticity, transparency, and quality, today's makers and entrepreneurs are driven to redefine excellence. They're fueled by a passion for their product, an entrepreneurial fire, and a desire to build a better world—all while meeting their own standards for self-fulfillment along the way.

I am living proof that success is possible, despite the remarkably high bar that's been set. And with the benefit of the know-how that took me over seven years to amass, I'm offering this book as a springboard to supermakers like you. I've put it all in these pages, from my days hand-pouring deodorant in the kitchen to heading up a 150-employee company. This book contains not just my own story, but all the lessons I learned along the way. My hope is that it will help you bypass years of toil or self-doubt, so you too can embrace and become the supermaker you are.

Part I

Make It

Yours

Perfect your product
+ share your passion

CHAPTER 1

Don't quit the quest.

Seek out your "thing"; you'll know when you've found it.

I had no idea what I was doing. I was thirty-one years old, eight months pregnant, in a wonderful but still very new relationship, and working a job that didn't suit me. Mostly, I was in a rush to figure out who I was, and quickly, before beginning my new, unexpected role of mother. So there I was, stirring up my first batch of deodorant in the kitchen of my tiny rental in Portland.

From the moment I started making, that kitchen was a disaster. The oils and butters gunked up every surface, and the sink was a few days away from being completely clogged. There were crumpled-up papers of discarded recipes and notes littered across the counter. Essential oils and samples of my latest test batches cluttered every inch of surface space available, alongside my jars of homemade kombucha and hot sauce. My feet ached from standing, and I was already tired after long days at my full-time job. As I stirred, bigger questions swirled around my head: *Am I ready to be a mother? Should I stay in this job? Will we have enough money?* And an old, familiar one: *What's my purpose?*

But something about the process of making put my world in order (even as it sent my kitchen into disarray). Only one thing was certain: the very act of creating—leaning over my kitchen stove, mixing the butters and powders and essential oils, pouring the mixture carefully into little Mason jars—lit me up like nothing else had before.

I was not one of those kids who "always knew" she was a writer or a musician or a doctor or an artist. I spent years thinking, *I don't know what my passion is*, or simply, *I don't have a passion*. I was searching for it, but I also didn't know where to look. I kept trying to figure out where I belonged, time and again, working odd jobs, moving from one city to another, enrolling in classes, only to find myself at a lot of dead ends. In that Portland kitchen, I was lucky enough to discover something—and once I did, I kept at it, relentlessly.

Perhaps not surprisingly, I didn't set out with deodorant as my destination.

I grew up in a tiny Bavarian tourist town in Michigan—population fewer than five thousand—where you could (and still can) dial 1-800-FUNTOWN to call the chamber of commerce. My dad worked as an engineer for General Motors and my mom stayed home to raise me and my older brother, Jason. My family has always been close and very supportive (and to this day we talk regularly), though I wouldn't say that we shared a lot of deep, emotional conversations growing up. Ours was a relatively reserved household, where we were more likely to talk about local news and the weather than our inner feelings or aspirations.

I count myself as very fortunate to have experienced a childhood of freedom in the company of a loving family. I spent many hours playing with my best friends—two girls who lived down the street—riding bikes around the neighborhood loop and exploring the woods, which we called "Wonderland." We'd play in the creeks and catch crawfish; climb trees and pick flowers. We spent whole afternoons in our treehouse, inventing stories and imagining other worlds.

On weekends, my parents, my brother, and I would visit my grandparents in northern Michigan. They lived on a lake, where we'd fish in summer and play on the ice in winter. We called the surrounding area the "Deep Dark Woods," though it was wondrous and welcoming. I'd walk around collecting acorns, putting them all in a Ziploc bag my grandmother gave me. Back home, I'd dump them out, play with them, then return them to their bag for later—my own little treasures.

When it came time for college, I followed in my brother's footsteps and attended Michigan State University, a Big Ten school notorious for its athletics and fraternity/sorority scene. I roomed with my best friend from high school, Anne, who already knew she wanted to major in political science and move to Washington, DC, after graduation. I didn't have a clear sense of what I wanted to be when I grew up. My brother had majored in business, so I did the same, though I wasn't passionate about it. That lack of pride and confidence in what I was doing felt like a heavier weight each year I carried it with me. Any time I was asked "What's your major?" I hated trying to fake my way into a good reason for why I'd chosen business.

Between classes, I worked. For a while I was a student ID checker and dishwasher in the dorm cafeteria. Later I became a sandwich maker at a Blimpie sub shop, then moved on up to kitchen prep and cook at a kitschy chain restaurant. I wanted to be a server, but first had to climb the ranks, which included dressing up as the restaurant's mascot and standing roadside during rush hour. After one too many days sweating in my costume, I decided it was time to quit. Eventually I landed a server position at the local Chi-Chi's, the Mexican food chain, where I developed a rapport with the regulars, who racked up higher tabs (and higher tips) as they drank.

As graduation approached, I somewhat hastily added a minor in human resources. The inevitability of facing the "real world" was on the horizon, and I didn't have a clue about what I was going to do with my business degree once I was out there. Human resources seemed somewhat interesting; at least it involved humans, as opposed to the world of numbers and data I had been immersed in with my business classes.

I got the feeling that my future was supposed to look something like this: graduate from a good college, work a steady job, get married, and "settle down." Where was the fun part? I'd rather go back to the Deep Dark Woods and collect acorns. But I carried on that path, taking steps that I thought were supposed to lead me to happiness.

When I graduated, I moved in with my boyfriend, who had a summer job working in landscaping, while I, after months of sending out dozens of applications, started working at a small, privately owned staffing company. My boss was erratic and once screamed at me for giving someone's paycheck to their mom instead of directly to the employee. She told me her boss would have thrown an ashtray at her head for such reckless behavior. That job didn't last long.

A string of other jobs at different staffing companies followed, and eventually my boyfriend and I moved to Chicago, where finally I got what felt like a "real" HR job at a gas technology company. While it was thrilling to live in Chicago, I still felt lost in my career. I went back to school for a master's in sociology. I wasn't sure exactly how I'd use the degree, but I hoped it would expand my qualifications and opportunities for some future role that would resonate with me. My employer helped fund the degree, and I stuck it out over the next three years, juggling the commute, job, and classes after work.

I was hustling along the prescribed path but continued to feel unfulfilled. My boyfriend and I agreed it was time to take the next step in our relationship, and we got married. Soon after, we bought our first home, a condo in downtown Chicago that seemed like a smart investment. I left the gas tech company to work at the prestigious MacArthur Foundation. Their office was located in downtown Chicago and commuting by train each day felt like a luxurious upgrade, after making the long haul by car to my previous office in the suburbs.

From the outside, life looked good: great city, new husband, home, master's degree, and fancy job. But something still felt off. On my commute to work, I'd look around at the faces of strangers on the train, thinking everyone seemed tired and burnt out. At the office, the monotony of giving new-hire orientations quickly became tedious, and I always felt like a schmuck reviewing staid policies and procedures with employees who had more important work to do. I couldn't shake a persistent feeling of discontent. I knew there had to be something more, but I didn't know how to go about finding it. To make matters worse, I was having the same feeling about my marriage.

One day at work, my boss and I dialed into a conference call together in her office. When it was my turn to speak, I didn't recognize myself. My voice sounded unusually strained and shaky, dipping and rising, making it difficult to be understood. When the call ended, I looked at her and said, "What's happening to my voice?"

"You sound nervous," she responded, but I wasn't feeling nervous at all.

The "voice thing" happened more and more. My voice would become shaky for seemingly no reason, and I was unable to control it. It was a blow to my confidence, and it was scary. What was happening to me? I began scheduling appointments with doctors. It took a long time and many visits before we discovered what it was: spasmodic dysphonia, a rare neurological condition that causes vocal cords to spasm. While that sounded terrifying, the doctor reassured me that the condition wasn't a threat to my health. There wasn't anything I could do about it, either. Not much was known about its cause or cure, as the condition is so rare. I just had to carry on.

Much later I learned that trauma or stress can trigger spasmodic dysphonia. Coming across that information made me wonder if I had become so deeply unhappy in my life in Chicago that this was my body's way of insisting I make a change.

I'll never be sure exactly what the impetus was, but I did make a change. My husband was feeling as restless as I was. Were we both unhappy in our careers, or were we feeling trapped in our relationship, having met and married so young? We agreed on one thing: we'd move across the country and make a fresh start. Portland, Oregon, was our city of choice. We'd visited, and we loved the impression we got of the young, energetic people who lived there. There was easy access to hiking trails and camping sites. It seemed like the perfect change of pace and scenery from our life in the Midwest. After five years in Chicago, we sold the condo and, like many seekers before us, headed West. Neither of us had a job lined up, but with the money from the sale of the condo we had some security, along with the faith we'd find our way.

"This job is so not you"

I loved Portland right away. It felt like a small big city—the perfect size—and it notably lacked Chicago's cold weather and chaotic traffic patterns. It seemed like there was a real community there. I just needed to find my way in.

With the move, I was determined to start fresh in my career. But how? I didn't have any connections and couldn't afford to put off working for long. I resigned myself to getting another job in HR, promising myself that it would only be temporary.

I found a job with Portland Public Schools giving orientations to new teachers and administering their benefits packages, working alongside a small group of primarily female coworkers. Our desks were practically within arm's reach of each other, so we'd get talking about our lives—friendly chatter to pass the time. One day one of my colleagues looked at me warmly and said, "This job is *so* not you." She didn't mean it in a critical way, and I wasn't offended. It was validating to know that someone else could sense my internal confusion; someone else recognized that I didn't belong. Just like each job I'd held in my twenties, this was a valuable part of my journey, bringing new relationships, lessons, and skills, teaching me what I *didn't* want. But I still couldn't see through the fog. What job *was* for me? What *did* I want?

As part of my new-city adventure, I bought a moped. The fuel-efficient scooters were popular in Portland at the time, and I figured if I was going to commute to this office every day, I might as well have some fun doing it. The first time I tried to mount the bike, it fell on top of me. I picked it up and thought, *Bring it on.* I was determined to stake my claim to a newfound sense of freedom and fun.

It was liberating to be untethered from Chicago's train schedule, and instead to zip through the quiet, tree-lined streets of Portland. It was the rainy season, but that didn't deter me. I bought a water-resistant jacket with padded elbows, along with lined waterproof pants and boots. I completed my all-black outfit with a burgundy helmet. I'd arrive at work and pull into the motorcycle section of the lot around back, where typically I was the only woman.

That fall, despite the fact that we'd taken this leap of faith together, found jobs, and tried to make a fresh start, my husband and I decided to end our relationship. We'd followed all the steps we thought we were supposed to and had even shaken things up by moving West. But we had to be honest with ourselves and each other: it was time to go our separate ways. Deep down, I knew we weren't the right fit. I remember sitting on our bed and realizing that I was about to be truly alone for the first time in my adult life. I was terrified. And what would my parents think? I already felt like I'd let them down by uprooting my "settled" life in Chicago and turning from a perfectly laid-out path. But much to my relief, they were both very supportive and nonjudgmental. Soon after I told my mom, she said, "Well, I guess we can get rid of that old wedding dress and the photos we've been storing!" (She hates clutter.)

Now it was just me and my moped. I moved into a small one-bedroom apartment on the top floor of an old house. I was living alone for the first time in my life, in a new city where I knew almost no one. It was a difficult and confusing time, but also an invigorating one. I felt a new sense of possibility. I remember buying a big bookcase from IKEA and sitting on the floor one night, a glass of wine in hand, music playing in the background, slowly assembling the thing myself. It took hours and hours, but I did it. The world was mine.

A new friend invited me to join a sewing class with her. If I couldn't find satisfaction in a job, maybe a side project could fill the void. For the first few classes, I was so excited. I had visions of starting a business by giving new life to thrifted clothes, like turning men's collared shirts into dresses. I wrote a mission statement and found a clip art image of a lotus flower (symbolizing rebirth) for my logo. I went to the thrift store and bought a bunch of pieces with every intention of reinventing and reselling them. I bought my own sewing machine and got to work.

The following Saturday, I spent the entire day stitching a simple tube dress from a pattern. For hours I sat bent over my machine. At the end of the day, the seams were all crooked, and one of the arms was lower than the other. It was completely unwearable. I was exhausted and—worst of all—uninspired. Not long after, I gave up on sewing. The fire inside me just wasn't there.

Other attempts at finding a creative outlet were just as short-lived. I bought a little kit and explored wood carving, etching the word "DAD" into a block and sending it to him. It looked like a four-year-old crafted it, and we laugh about it now, though it still hangs above his workbench in the basement. I enrolled in classes at a local community college in pursuit of yet another degree—this time in interior design, in the hopes of starting my own firm. But I ultimately ended the degree program early. I was asked to give a presentation in front of the class, which made me uncomfortable because of my voice condition, but more notably, I realized my heart wasn't in it. I lacked the drive to push forward.

I was racking up "failed" attempts at finding my passion, but at least one thing was clear: I had a creative urge that needed an outlet. I had promised myself the HR job would be temporary, and a year later, I needed to deliver on that. I still didn't know what my true calling was (or even if I had one), but I figured if I had a different job—out in the world instead of spending monotonous days stuck in a cubicle—it could help me transition into whatever I was *really* meant to do.

Though there were a ton of service jobs in Portland, they were very competitive and difficult to land. At the time, the city was known as the place where twenty-somethings moved to "retire" and get by with a restaurant or bartending job. I'd had a whole career in HR since my service days at Chi-Chi's. But when I saw a listing for Zach's Shack, a hot dog joint not too far from my apartment on the southeast side of the city, I went for it. I needed a change. If it had to be hot dogs, so be it.

"Shack" really was an accurate name. There were no more than eight little tables and a small bar up front, managed by a single bartender, and a cooking station in the back, managed by the cook: me. I'd stand there in my apron, sweating and covered in grease (there was no A/C), constantly making sure the buns were steamed to the perfect softness, the hot dogs were plentiful, and the fries were hot.

The busiest time was 1:00 A.M. After the bars closed, tipsy twenty-somethings would come flooding in for a late-night dog and a nightcap, and the line often stretched out the door. During my ten-or-so-hour shift, I prepped the hot dogs and toppings, assembled orders in red plastic baskets, carried them up to the bar, and called out in my often broken or strained voice over the drunken conversation, "Vegan dog for Joe! Joe! *JOE!*" It was a scene. By the time I got home after a shift and peeled off my grease-soaked, hot dog–smelling clothes and collapsed into bed, the sun would be coming up.

You'll feel when you've found it

I was thirty years old, newly divorced, and working at a hot dog shack. However that looked on paper, I felt like I was moving forward—something new was on the horizon; I could feel it. I still had some savings left from when I first moved to Portland, and I used them to set out on a soul-searching road trip across America, racking up 120 hours of driving time and stopping off at roadside motels whenever I was ready for a break (not long after the divorce, I'd sold the moped for a used Saab). Neither the trip nor the subsequent silent meditation retreat I attended provided any immediate answers, but they helped me see I was ready to take ownership over the next chapter of my life. Upon returning to Portland, I reminded myself that Zach's was yet another "transition" job and refocused on my goal to pursue more meaningful, sustainable work.

I returned to the job listings and spotted a position at a residential facility for children with behavioral and mental health issues. The company was seeking entry-level candidates with degrees in psychology. I wondered if my master's in sociology was a close-enough fit. I'd grown up babysitting and loved working with kids, and this sounded like a job that would actually be challenging and fulfilling. (However, working with these kids, many of whom had serious mental health and medical diagnoses, would prove very different from the babysitting I'd done in my teenage years.) The starting pay was very low—around ten dollars an hour—and the position seemed to be geared toward recent college graduates. But I knew I'd have to go back to an entry-level role if I really wanted to restart my career, so I applied. What did I have to lose?

By this point, I'd held dozens of jobs and was skilled at interviewing. However, with the onset of my vocal condition, interviews weren't as breezy as they used to be, and I began to dread them. Getting nervous only made it worse. Thankfully, even though my professional experience wasn't an ideal match, the interview went well enough, and I was offered the job. My colleagues were all young, eager, and dedicated to the work. I was energized and inspired by their dedication. I worked from 1:00 P.M. to 10:00 P.M. Many of the employees regularly met up after work to unwind. One of our favorite bars was a dive named Lotsa Luck Bar & Grill, with an old-school jukebox. We would all cram around a little table to download about the day over sweaty glasses of beer. I'd lived in Portland for just over a year, and my life was starting to have a sense of order. I liked the meaningfulness of this new job and my fledgling group of coworker friends. I'd moved apartments again and was living in a tiny studio that felt cozy. For the first time in a long while, I felt like I had some sense of community. I put "figuring things out" on pause and allowed myself to enjoy being exactly where I was. I was at home. And right around this time, I met Chris.

He was only in his mid-twenties, but Chris, a coworker, was extremely skilled at his job and was already a supervisor. He had a quiet confidence and comforting demeanor about him that we all appreciated. In one of my early days on the job, he and I were working in the same residential unit when a little girl made a mess of the bathroom. Poop was smeared all over the bathtub and floor—it was everywhere. As the new hire, cleanup duties like this fell to me. As I gagged and mentally prepared myself for the task at hand, Chris turned to me and said, "Let's do it together." He grinned, adding, "It'll be fun!"

That was Chris. He was laid-back and friendly, with a mop of wavy dark hair and kind blue eyes. That night at happy hour, we both found ourselves leaning over the juke-box, connecting over a shared love of experimental pop classics and rap music. Within a week we were burning mix CDs for each other. Soon after that, we began dating.

One Saturday early in our relationship, Chris and I went to an arts festival by the river in downtown Portland. It was late morning and I was sipping a cup of coffee as we walked. Suddenly, I felt incredibly nauseated. That was unusual for me, especially because I drank coffee regularly and prided myself on having a stomach of steel. Something was going on. I looked at Chris and managed to tell him we needed to go buy a pregnancy test—*now*. We walked to a pharmacy, then drove back to my studio apartment. I took the test, then we sat on the bed and waited.

I'll never forget the moment. I went back to the tiny bathroom and brought out the test. I sat down, shoulder to shoulder with Chris, and we both looked down at the plastic stick. I was pregnant. We had only been dating for six months. A scary, overwhelming sensation washed over me. But underneath it, somehow, there was also a deep, abiding confidence that this was going to be okay—in fact, that this was *right*. I just knew. Chris immediately said, "Let's do this."

In the coming months, we moved in together and became engaged. As my belly grew, Chris and I found a rhythm in our new life together. I didn't for a moment second-guess the relationship or our decision; I felt happy and excited for the future.

And yet, that old nagging question persisted: *What's my purpose?* I looked forward to becoming a mother. I knew that new role would challenge and hopefully fulfill me like nothing else—but it didn't erase my longing for an independent, creative passion; it only intensified it. If someone asked, "What do you do?" I wanted to be able to talk about my skills and my passion with pride. I knew being able to do that was a gift I'd be giving my future child, too.

There were many things I loved about my job, but it wasn't sustainable. The pay was very low, and I lacked the specialized training needed for growth, including how to work with children with complex conditions and aggressive behaviors. In my first trimester, I transitioned into more of an administrative role where I had less direct contact with the children. Completely exhausted, I'd close the door to my office, use my coat as a pillow, and take a nap. At the end of the day, I'd come home feeling drained and dissatisfied. Chris often left the house to play with his punk band (which was gaining popularity), leaving me to wonder about my own calling.

It was 2010, and the Maker Movement was going strong in Portland. Everyone in our group of friends seemed to be committed to some kind of a creative endeavor. I admired the way everyone around me seemed to maintain passion projects—they were artists, jewelry designers, musicians— and I yearned for something to call my own.

One day, as I sat in my office, alone with my thoughts, I looked down at my growing belly and wondered about the tiny being inside. I was seven months pregnant. Soon my world would change with no going back. Was time running out to make my mark as Jaime Schmidt? I turned to my computer and googled "classes in Portland." I scrolled through the results, unimpressed. I'd tried random classes before and wanted something different. One entry caught my eye: a class called "DIY Shampoo," hosted by a woman on the northeast side of town. During my pregnancy, I'd been thinking a lot about how to eat well and use products that were safe for the baby. Portland was full of natural food stores and co-ops that stocked all things natural, and I'd become accustomed to checking labels and making conscious decisions about what to use on my body. Making my own shampoo sounded fun. Plus, Chris and I were on a lean budget, and it couldn't hurt to save a few bucks by making our own products. The class was that same night. I signed up.

It was raining when I left work. About ten of us, all women, showed up to the teacher's small home. Cheryl was roughly my age, and she seemed gentle, with a nurturing demeanor. We gathered around her while she stood at her stove. I maneuvered my big belly close to the front for the best view and watched as Cheryl carefully dropped calendula blossoms, chamomile buds, nettle, rosemary, and other herbs into a pot of boiling water, explaining each ingredient's purpose and benefits. A curl of steam wafted from the pot, and the kitchen filled with comforting herbal scents. I was enchanted. I wrote down everything Cheryl said, recording the ingredients, instructions, and every book recommendation for DIY beauty creations.

When it came time for Cheryl to divvy up her mixture, pouring a little bit into each attendee's bottle, I all but elbowed my way forward. A genuine fascination had awakened within me. It was instant, intuitive. Already I felt as if this was *my thing.* I went home with a newfound fire of inspiration I'd never felt before.

Soon I had a stack of books and was spending all of my after-work hours at the stove making soaps, shampoo bars, conditioners, lotions, foot creams, and tinctures. When I didn't get something right or when something went wrong, I wanted to tinker and figure it out, or start from scratch; the process kept my attention. This new passion for making natural personal care products consumed me. Any time I walked into a store, I found myself in that aisle, picking up soaps and shampoos, studying ingredients, and concocting a plan of how I could make my own better version. It was all I wanted to do.

While the books I brought home contained hundreds of pages dedicated to all varieties of tinctures and lotions, they listed just a few scant recipes for deodorant. I was surprised; deodorant was such an important part of daily body care, and I knew there were health concerns around some of the ingredients used in traditional formulations. I'd tried nearly every natural kind on the market (nearly all lavender scented) and was always let down by how ineffective they were. In fact, I'd given up entirely on natural deodorant and had resigned myself to using a stick of Soft & Dri. But now that I had made my own shampoo and conditioner, with my cabinets filling up with coconut oil and essential oils of all kinds, maybe I could solve this myself. Determined, I draped my apron over my swollen belly, tied it around my waist, and got to work. I didn't know it yet, but in that kitchen, while I waited for one new life to come into the world, another legacy was about to be born, too. ∎

What to make of it

 Knowing what you're passionate about is more than half the battle.

If you're already there, take a moment to celebrate that. Seriously. This book is about turning that passion into profit, and there's a lot to cover. For now, I want you to appreciate where you are.

 Explore!

If you're in the unsure-what-my-passion-is realm and experimenting, exploring, and seeking—that's great, too! Keep going. Trust your curiosity. Get your hands dirty. Pay attention to what gives you joy. Give yourself time to search for, find, and cultivate what you're passionate about. You deserve a creative life. We all do.

 "Success" looks different for everybody, so you have to define it for yourself.

Some makers don't want to turn their passion into a business, or at least not into a *big* business, and I respect that. Simply having a passion is its own reward. And for many people, it's enough. For me, once I finally found a skill I could call my own—something I could create with passion and share with pride—I wanted to make it a bigger part of my life. The most important thing is for you to be in tune with what success means to *you*. Give yourself the room to let that evolve over time. You might surprise yourself. I sure did.

CHAPTER 2

Get your hands dirty.

Jump in, hone your process, and commit to your product.

M aking deodorant is almost like preparing a complex meal. In the beginning, I'd come home from work, put on a beat-up pair of Skechers, tie my apron, and stand at the stove for hours, stirring. I took notes in a greasy journal and typed them up later, keeping track of what was working and what wasn't.

I researched, experimented, tried, and tried again to create something great. The first deodorant I created wasn't fancy (I started with just one scent in a Mason jar) and wasn't final (I continued to tweak the formula along the way). Before I even considered selling it to anyone, I made sure it was better than anything else I'd tried.

Today I can look back and see that my insistence on excellence was what laid the foundation for all that Schmidt's would become. Striving for your own standard of excellence is another thing that I find makers intuitively understand. Makers are on a mission to create something *amazing*. We're in love with our product. We believe in it fiercely. That's the whole reason we're sharing it, selling it, investing in it, growing it. A dedication to our own high standards—and a passion and love for the process—is precisely why the Maker Movement has become a *movement*.

However, that doesn't mean creating a high-quality product is straightforward. Makers are faced with tough decisions about just what "high quality" means to them and about what it will take to achieve. What if the materials are simply too expensive? What if your efforts land you in an endless research and development phase, preventing you from putting your product out there? What if you *have* put yourself out there, and the feedback you're getting isn't what you expected? What if a major life event (for me, it was the birth of my son) takes place in the middle of your product development journey? Now what?

Makers have to contend with all kinds of what-ifs along the way, plus difficult cost-benefit analyses, integrity questions, personal circumstances, and product challenges. I've been through it. And while the way you make these decisions is personal and there will rarely be a single "right" answer, I've found that getting clear about what excellence means to you—and then returning to that commitment time and again—pays off. And it all begins by committing to your product, taking a deep breath, and jumping in.

Be patient (not perfect) with the process

Of all the products I was learning to make, deodorant was the most exciting to me; probably because it was the most challenging to get right. But I was determined to ditch my

Soft & Dri and come up with a natural formula that smelled amazing, looked beautiful, felt great to the touch, and actually *worked*. I've always had a sensitive nose. I was aware of subtle aromas like fallen leaves and offended by chemical scents like air fresheners—which meant I was constantly conscious of how I smelled. My standards were high.

Most deodorant recipes in my new DIY books were vinegar based, meant to be spritzed. Was that really going to cut it? I was skeptical. I also didn't find the idea of spraying my pits with vinegar to be very appealing.

I took my research endeavors online, where I learned that milk of magnesia was a popular deodorant ingredient. Its high pH value neutralized acidic odor-causing bacteria, and it was historically known to help with body odor. However, it was typically used in a liquid deodorant, which I thought would feel sticky and wet. I wanted to create something smooth, soft, and matte.

That brought me to "solid" deodorant recipes, which varied widely. I realized quickly that achieving a smooth texture and perfect consistency—while also achieving a shelf-stable product without synthetics—wouldn't be easy. Most conventional deodorants contain propylene glycol to give deodorant the glide we're accustomed to. Most also have a high water content, as water acts as a filler that keeps costs low. However, using water also means having to include synthetic preservatives that prevent bacterial growth. It was important to me that every ingredient would benefit the skin or contribute to the effectiveness of the product, and I had no interest in incorporating water, fillers, or controversial ingredients.

One of the first recipes I tried out was simply coconut oil and baking soda. I loved the simplicity of it but realized that the texture was unpredictable. The coconut oil was solid when cool but had a very low melting point, and mixing it with baking soda resulted in a grainy, sandy feel. And the formula wasn't entirely effective at controlling odor.

I started experimenting with plant-based butters that would make my solution firm and smooth, like mango butter, almond butter, avocado butter, cocoa butter, and shea butter. Each had its own scent, texture, and melting point, with large variations in cost. I also started adding cornstarch, which I discovered acted similarly to baking soda in helping control odor and leaving the underarms feeling fresh. And I incorporated vitamin E for its antioxidant properties that could help prolong shelf life.

The more difficult part was determining what proportion of each ingredient to use—did I need more baking soda, less cornstarch? Less shea butter, more cocoa butter? And then how should I combine them to achieve a smooth, effective end result? I realized that the melting and cooling processes significantly impacted how the final product turned out. Sometimes I'd end up with a little jar with oil sitting on top and powders sunk to the bottom. Other times the formula was lumpy, or dried well at first, then became spotty on top a day or two later. The weather mattered, too, especially when working in a home without AC. If it was cold out, the butter would be harder and take longer to melt; if it was warm, the opposite occurred. My first experiments showed the butters would melt in ten minutes at 300°F (150°C). But I learned some days I didn't need the full ten minutes, and if I let the product get too hot, that affected how it mixed with the other ingredients and how the final, cooled consistency turned out.

Texture was one of my biggest initial challenges. To understand how each ingredient was impacting the texture of the final, cooled deodorant, I'd isolate different factors. In one night, I might make five batches of deodorant. Each batch made four jars, so I'd end up with twenty total. I'd keep all the ingredients and steps in the process steady, but only change the amount of cocoa butter from one batch to the next. I'd set the deodorants out to cool for twenty-four hours, labeling each batch A, B, C, D, and E with corresponding notes, then wait to see how the texture turned out. For the ones that looked good, I'd test that version for multiple days to know how well it worked. A few days later I'd start over again, this time maybe only adjusting the amount of baking soda or the mixing temperature. It seemed the ratios of ingredients I could try were endless, and the process was continually evolving. I would continue to revisit this time-intensive procedure many times in the future, refining it along the way as I developed new formulations. Eventually I'd share the process with contract manufacturers, who traditionally had only ever produced deodorants with a much different ingredient profile and would adopt and adapt my process for large-scale manufacturing.

Chris was happy to see me so passionate about my new project, and he was always encouraging, no matter what the kitchen looked like. He also became a guinea pig for my creations. Each of us would go about our days with different variations of deodorant under each arm. When he got home from work, I'd pull him toward me and put my nose under his arm to see how it had held up, and this became a normal part of our daily routine. Lucky for me, Chris was game to try everything. From the moment I brought home a jar of shampoo I'd made in Cheryl's class, Chris used it on his hair, too, along with a vinegar rinse conditioner I made soon after. He'd come shuffling out of the bathroom plucking rosemary sprigs out of his hair, telling me how much he enjoyed the rinse. Having his support motivated me even more. When I started making cold-process bar soap with a book called *How to Make Soap: Without Burning Your Face Off*, he was a bit wary, but still trusted and supported me. The process required lye, which was dangerous if not handled appropriately, so we kept it out in our garage in a bucket with a cute skull and crossbones illustration drawn by yours truly.

I was so excited and proud of what I was making—these soaps, shampoos, conditioners, lotions, and, hopefully soon, the perfect deodorant—that I began dreaming of sharing my creations. Portland had a vibrant farmers market scene, and I could picture myself there. What would I call my creations? One night when we had friends over, we sat around and brainstormed names. We tried versions of "Jaime's," but in the end "Schmidt's"—a common, familiar name—stood out as the strongest. Plus, many of my friends called me "Schmidt" at the time. I hadn't always been fond of it (think of what rhymes with Schmidt or Schmidty in the mind of teenagers), but for now I just needed something to call my fun project. I had no idea that I'd one day be seeing that name—*my* name—splashed across TV screens, in magazines, and on shelves at Target.

What's in a name?

QUICK TIPS TO CONSIDER WHEN NAMING YOUR BUSINESS

Simplicity. In general, the fewer syllables, the better.

Originality. Imagine your name alongside the competition. If it sounds at all like the rest, ditch it.

Room to grow. If you get too specific, your name may not fit as your business evolves. This happened at Schmidt's; we had to change our name from Schmidt's Deodorant to Schmidt's Naturals to make room for other product lines. For us, it was a pretty easy transition since our biggest name recognition was for "Schmidt's."

Appearance. Think about the way the name will look on the packaging, in ads, and as a logo. Play around with design to help you decide.

Trademark infringements. I've known entrepreneurs who have received notices of trademark violation because the name of their business was too similar to a competing brand already on the market. Consider hiring an attorney to do trademark research on your behalf; it's worth it.

Legacy. If you name the brand after yourself, you just might be solidifying your legacy forever. Today, I'm happy this was the decision I made.

My friend Rick, a graphic designer and former coworker at my job with the kids, offered to help me create a logo. He took a picture of me wearing a bonnet purchased for $9.99 on Amazon (I wanted to go with a homestead vibe that was trendy at the time) and turned it into a pioneer-style illustration of me with "Schmidt's" across the top. After some back and forth to perfect my face, I could hardly contain my excitement when I saw his finished drawing.

Meanwhile, I was nine months pregnant and increasingly concerned about my upcoming delivery, as the baby had moved into a breech position and I desperately hoped to avoid a C-section. Making was put on pause while I tried all the tricks in the book (and then some) to move him out of breech position, from standing on my head, to burning candles at my pinky toes (a form of moxibustion), to visits at the doctor where they physically tried to turn the baby from the outside of my stomach. On the morning of January 11, 2010, a few days past my due date, I went in for a regular checkup. The doctor was concerned that I was losing amniotic fluid and was adamant that the birth needed to happen that day. As she led me to the birthing unit in a wheelchair, Chris raced home to grab my overnight bag that had been sitting patiently by the door for weeks. The C-section went smoothly, and at 12:47 P.M., Chris cut the umbilical cord and little Oliver Wylee entered our world.

Chris and I fell instantly and deeply in love with the tiny being now entrusted into our care. I remember watching him sleep in the bassinet next to our bed, knowing he was the best thing to ever happen in my life. Yet Oliver's presence also stoked a real sense of urgency to find out if I could make my business idea a reality—now for him, as much as for myself.

During Oliver's naps, I'd creep into the kitchen and work on my formulas, careful not to make too much noise, as his room was right off the kitchen. I was exhausted, but also too inspired to rest, and nap times were the only opportunities I had to really focus. Thankfully, he slept on a predictable schedule, allowing me a few hours to work in the morning and again in the afternoon. Sometimes just a few minutes after sneaking out, I'd creep right back into Oliver's room to stare at his tiny, swaddled body, till I saw his chest rise and was reassured he was breathing. Like all new mothers, I was constantly nervous about his well-being.

Back in the kitchen, I returned to mixing and cooling at different intervals, trying to get the deodorant just right. Finally, after months at work—the countertops strewn with ingredients and Oliver's bottles drying on the rack—and countless experiments on my own armpits (and Chris's), I nailed a version I loved. It was a combination of baking soda and cornstarch, shea butter and cocoa butter, and vitamin E oil. When cooled, it was creamy white, solid, and smooth. It warmed and softened on my fingertips when I scooped it and spread easily on my underarms. And—to my amazement— it really, really worked.

With the deodorant recipe nailed, I went on to finish formulating a lotion recipe—a combination of almond oil, emulsifying wax, vegetable glycerin, and olive oil. Next came scent exploration. Our laundry room closet filled up with tiny half-ounce bottles of essential oils of every variety. With smells wafting from behind the closed doors, just walking into the room was a sensory experience. Whenever friends came over, I'd ask them to smell one oil, and then one added to another, and on and on. I learned that some oils were much more potent than others; that some were more polarizing while others were crowd-pleasing; and that some mixed well with my formulas while others fell flat. After countless rounds of experimenting, I chose just one for the deodorant: cedarwood. It was an affordable and differentiating essential oil, and one that I absolutely loved, both because I personally prefer woody scents, and because it was so different from anything else used in deodorant at the time. It felt unexpected, unique, and appealing—especially for the Pacific Northwest, known for its expansive, beautiful forests.

With the lotions, I imagined people wanting a variety of scents, so I got playful with more options. I expected people would want a citrus option, so I chose grapefruit. Lavender is popular, but I wanted to be different, so I added cypress. I also made a "rainy day" rosemary (inspired by spring in Portland), sweet orange patchouli, and a fragrance-free option. With each, I was careful to achieve what I considered the perfect amount of scent—not too subtle, but not overwhelming.

And just like that, nearly six months after attending Cheryl's shampoo class, I had my first line of products.

Can you turn your hobby into a business?

CONSIDERATIONS BEFORE TURNING YOUR PASSION INTO A BUSINESS

Scalability. Can your product be made at a high volume in a cost-effective manner? Producing larger and larger deodorant batches posed its own set of challenges, but it was a huge advantage that I was able to increase production as the business grew.

Demand. Is there a market for your product? Are people hungry for it and willing to pay? Sometimes it takes a trial run (like what I did initially at local markets) to find out.

Motivation. Running a business takes ambition and a competitive spirit. While I didn't have a formal plan, I quickly became devoted to expanding.

Monetization. Calculate whether you can sell your products for more than they cost to make. And consider whether you can bring costs down over time, e.g., buying ingredients in bulk at a discount. Find out your COGS (cost of goods sold) by adding up all the costs that go into making a single product, like the cost of materials used and direct labor costs. (This calculation will vary depending on your product and business, and might also include other costs like warehouse space, administrative tasks, etc.) Your COGS is deducted from revenue to calculate gross profit.

Support. Who can help you? Who can cheer you on? Sustaining a business requires ongoing support from family and friends, fellow entrepreneurs, and community members.

Take your business seriously, and others will follow suit

As my maternity leave ended, Chris and I agreed it made better sense for me to find a new part-time job instead of going back to work at the children's facility—as long as it paid more than the cost of a caregiver. We both wanted me to have as much time at home with Oliver as possible. My previous experience was just relevant enough for me to land a part-time position at a company that built housing for low-income communities. It paid well enough, and the office included a room where I could pump for breastfeeding. For Oliver's care, we found a warm, doting woman in the neighborhood who watched children at her home for a reasonable rate.

In the little downtime I had, I continued to perfect my formulations and prepared to get out and sell Schmidt's for the first time. I went to the local grocery store, Fred Meyer, and bought twenty-four-packs of Mason jars (small ones for the deodorant and larger ones for the lotion) and then took the homestead logo my friend Rick designed and printed labels at OfficeMax. I got an oversized hole punch and punched the labels into circles that could be stuck on top of the jars. Then I poured my lotions—Rainy Day Rosemary, Griffy's Grapefruit (named for a close friend), Into the Woods, Sweet Orange Patchouli, Lavender Cypress, and Fragrance Free—into large Mason jars, and my cedarwood deodorant into small ones. I did my own research, including spending a lot of time in the deodorant aisle every time I stepped into a grocery store, and settled on prices I felt were reasonable: six dollars for the deodorant and eight dollars for the lotion.

I asked Chris to help me set up a simple website (he was a talented designer and had been building websites since junior high), and we chose the domain SchmidtsBeauty .com. I also made a Schmidt's Facebook page and encouraged all my friends to follow. I began posting DIY recipes and links to articles, eager to prove I was a knowledgeable resource in the area. At work, I handed out jars of deodorant to colleagues and asked them to tell me what they thought.

I emailed organizers of farmers markets and street fairs across Portland, introducing myself as a local maker of all-natural body products. Most got back to me saying they were out of space—it was early summer, and markets were already booked up—or that they only hosted food vendors, or that I simply wasn't a good fit.

I was undeterred. Portland was full of little mom-and-pop shops that stocked local goods, and I reached out to those, too. There were a couple on my side of town: Local Goods and One Stop Sustainability Shop (the names tell you all you need to know). To my total surprise and delight, they both said they'd stock my deodorant and lotion on consignment (you give your product to a store and earn the money back once they sell). They liked that the products were unique, natural, and locally made. Polly, the manager at Local Goods, would become an early trusted advisor, someone I could talk with about pricing and other decisions down the line.

When I finally heard back from a street fair that accepted me, I was thrilled. I went to the thrift store and found a table-cloth (actually a quilted blanket to match the homestead vibe of my labels) and a card table. I wrote little blurbs about each of my products. From my research, I'd learned that cedarwood oil is known to be antiseptic and detoxifying, and I named that as a benefit. I also wrote that the deodorant neutralized odor and wetness and added a few other "claims" (that I learned, much later, could potentially pose a problem without "scientific" support, even if I was confident about the statements). I made a checklist of everything to bring the day of the event: my table, tablecloth, and sign; an envelope of cash to make change; and of course, lots of deodorant and lotion. As time went on, my checklist grew longer and longer as I added items like a notebook for news-letter sign-ups, business cards, shelves for the deodorant, tester sticks, signage, and sprigs of cedar for decoration.

Labels, logos, and smart design

THEY'RE AN EXTENSION OF YOUR PRODUCT—BE SURE THEY STAND OUT AND SAY THE RIGHT THINGS

Invest in your design. It's the first thing your customers see, and it's got to pop. If you need to keep costs down in the beginning like I did, work with a friend or local designer you can negotiate with, or even arrange a trade for the work, and prepare to invest as much of your own time as you can. I used to sit in bed at night sticking labels on jars, which actually became a pleasant way to relax and wind down.

Understand legal compliance. Know just what you need to say, legally, on those labels and tags. For a product like mine, that meant listing ingredients in a specific order and using a certain type size, including the place of manufacture, and, later, barcode compliance, along with a few other things.

Be wary of making claims. Later, I learned that saying an essential oil was "antiseptic and detoxifying" was the equivalent of making a medical claim, which could cause legal issues. This is true not just for labels, but in any marketing.

Consider a personal touch. When I first started selling online, I included one-line handwritten thank-you notes that I placed in shipping boxes. Customers appreciate knowing their order came from a real person.

Even though it was hot on the day of the street fair, I wore an old-timey dress and put on my bonnet so that I really looked the part. Chris had to work, so I brought Oliver (and my friend Jeni to help with him) and a playpen. I spread out my products, positioned my sign, and anxiously awaited the crowds. Despite the heat, they came. While bands played and artists performed nearby, the street became packed, and before long people were wandering up (partly enticed by cute Oliver), testing out my lotions and deodorants. Many were complimentary about how the scents were perfectly balanced. Some people actually put the deodorant right on their armpits, while others simply smelled or touched a sample and asked questions. I was aware of my voice sounding strained, but my excitement outweighed my nervousness, so I didn't get too self-conscious about it. Actually, I was having fun!

I don't remember the moment that I made my very first sale that day, but I do remember the mixed emotions that came with it. On one hand, I was completely elated. Here was something I'd researched, tested, and made myself in my own kitchen. I'd invested time and passion into it, and I knew it worked well—on me, at least. But would it work well for other people? Consumer testing groups were not yet in my realm of thinking. Standing on the other side of the table at that farmers market for the first time was a totally new, out-of-my-comfort-zone endeavor. Who did I think

I was, taking my home-brewed creations and selling them to strangers? It was actually pretty scary to step up and say, "Here's what I made and here's why you should buy it," especially when I wasn't sure it'd be successful. Did I have a right to take people's money in exchange for this Mason jar creation? Was my product worthy?

By the end of the day, my confidence was boosted and my comfort level had risen. Customers had been warm, curious, and supportive. And they'd *bought* deodorant and lotion. At one point I ran out of one-dollar bills and Jeni went to the bank for me, bringing back more so I could make change. There had been plenty of naysayers throughout the day, too—people with comments like, "Natural deodorant doesn't work"—but as the event rolled on, I found myself responding with a smile: "I guarantee this one does!" I even convinced a few skeptics that natural deodorant *can* work. When I got home, I burst through the door with Oliver in my arms and exclaimed to Chris, "People loved them!" I was beside myself. Only by putting myself out there did I begin to gain the confidence I needed to keep going. As I continued to show up, I learned more about how to make my products better.

Work your booth

HOW TO MAKE THE MOST OF MARKETS, FAIRS, AND LIVE EVENTS

Less is more. Customers should understand your business at a glance. Don't clutter your table with too many products, or a lot of materials they have to read.

Consider your location. See what you can do to work with show organizers to get a high-trafficked booth location. Sometimes I'd push my booth forward just slightly so I literally "stuck out" to passersby.

Give customers room to breathe. It's important to always acknowledge customers who approach and be ready to talk, but I've found that letting people initiate conversation puts them at ease; I never wanted to be too much in anyone's face.

Be prepared with conversation starters. "So, do you currently use a deodorant or antiperspirant? What brand? How is that working out for you?"

Sell bundles. As time went on, I realized how much people loved a good deal. I'd bundle my products (for example, buy three deodorants and get a discount) and people jumped at the chance to save a couple dollars.

Make friends with your booth neighbors. You just might want them to watch your booth when you need a bathroom break. Plus, trading builds community. My favorite trade was a jar of deodorant for a pint of blueberries at the farmers market.

Keep an email sign-up sheet. This is an essential way to build an early following.

Take photos. For social media, email newsletters, and your own memories!

Be warm, confident, and friendly with everyone. You never know who you'll meet.

I was a latecomer to the festival and market season that year, but I managed to land a spot at Montavilla Farmers Market a few weekends in October, as well as a spot at a popular festival called Muddy Boot. By then the weather had turned rainy and cool, and the markets weren't as well attended, but I continued to make sales and was consistently bolstered by the positive feedback I received from customers. I started bringing a sign-up sheet where passersby could leave their email address to receive updates (updates on what, I wasn't quite sure, but it seemed a smart business move). A day or two later, I sent a thank-you email to anyone who had stopped by the booth and signed up, inviting them to follow Schmidt's on Facebook and check out my retail locations on the website.

Meanwhile, the two local shops that stocked my deodorant and lotion let me know that I was selling a few products, and soon another local retailer, this time an ecommerce shop called Grow and Make, got back in touch with interest. I created an Etsy shop and loved how easy the platform was to use— not to mention the fact that it came with a built-in audience. I learned how important it was to stand out with high-quality photos, and how frequently relisting products and adding keyword-rich descriptions and tags helped me show up in search results. When my first orders came in, I was so thrilled and grateful that I felt the need to thank my customers personally. I'd write notes on the packing slips saying: "Thanks so much for your purchase, hope you enjoy! <3, Jaime." I kept up the practice as long as possible, until eventually I was selling so much deodorant that it became unsustainable.

Initially I didn't invest much time or energy into driving online sales. I had no formal budget at this point, including any allotted amount for advertising. Most of what I earned went back into ingredients and events, and it seemed like my efforts went further when I built relationships with customers at markets and with local shop owners who could help me gain traction in the Portland community.

One of the markets I'd emailed in the summer initially responded to say they strictly featured food and herbal remedies, but that I could follow up to apply for the craft festival held in the fall. I bookmarked the email and dutifully wrote again months later. "Since my initial email to you, my business has come a long way!" I wrote (I was learning the art of self-promotion). "My products are now on the shelves at Local Goods and The One Stop Sustainability Shop, both in Portland. I'll also be selling at the Muddy Boot Organic Festival. How might I have the opportunity to sell at People's Harvest Festival? Please visit my website to learn more about my business: www.schmidtsbeauty.com. Thank you!" It worked! I was so excited to be accepted, because the festival was hosted by a local co-op where I wasn't yet selling my products, and I thought this could be a foot in the door.

I was starting to realize that no one was going to take my business seriously before I did. Even though I was making products in my kitchen and pouring them into grocery store Mason jars, even though I still had a desk job, even though I didn't have *any* sort of business plan, even though from the outside it may have looked otherwise, I still considered myself an entrepreneur and called Schmidt's a business. Only because I took myself seriously could customers, shop owners, and market organizers do the same.

As fall turned to winter, I started scheming about how I could be better prepared for the next year. I spent more evenings and weekends in the kitchen expanding my product lines. I wanted to offer shampoo bars, conditioner spray, foot treatment bars, and sunscreen. I also updated my packaging, moving the products into aluminum tins and bottles that looked a little more refined than the Mason jars, and raised my prices. I worked on my pitch to market organizers and prepared to fill up my spring and summer weekends with markets and fairs across Portland and the surrounding suburbs.

When I think back to how brazen I was in the earliest stages of starting Schmidt's, I'm a little surprised. By nature, I'm more of an introvert who doesn't like to boast, and I hardly knew what I was doing, but my enthusiasm and pride for my creations propelled me into action. Once I started putting myself out there, the response I got from enthusiastic customers, shop owners, and market organizers made it easier to continue stepping up and taking myself and my fledgling business seriously. And the real-life relationships I formed in the process buoyed my work. People were getting to know and recognize me—I was cultivating a personal brand—and that created trust, which led to more opportunities. ■

What to make of it

 Keep your standards high.

It's all about the integrity of your product. Before you can think about brand personality, social media, or even *selling*, the first step is having an excellent product.

 But don't get stuck in perfectionism.

In the beginning, I kept things simple with my name, logo, prices, and even my booth, knowing this was just a starting point from which I could grow. Allow yourself this openness as you're starting out. Get your product as excellent as you can, then test drive it. As soon as your first customers (or friends or focus groups) experience what you have to offer, you'll get invaluable feedback that will get you to the next level.

 Get committed to fulfilling your creative needs.

I was fortunate to be able to carve out time for my new passion at the same time as I was starting a family, thanks to having a supportive partner and paid maternity leave. Ultimately, starting Schmidt's was about creating space for my own creativity and fulfillment, even during a transition period in my life when "responsibility" was taking on a whole new meaning. The juggle wasn't easy, and it only got harder, but it made me a more fulfilled person—and that made me a better parent *and* a better businessperson.

CHAPTER 3

Say yes now, then figure out how.

Cultivate an early following by listening to your community and seizing new opportunities.

I was enjoying growing my business from our 850-square-foot two-bedroom cottage. Chris continued with social work, and while his salary was low, the stability and security it provided kept our family afloat while I continued to work part time. His hours were unconventional, so most of the time one of us was home with the baby, and a couple days a week, Oliver was happy to spend time with the nanny neighbor. I loved watching him grow into a sweet, good-natured one-year-old who was almost always smiling and giggling. I'd taken out a loan from my dad when I attempted that interior design degree, and with the income from my part-time job, I was slowly paying him back in $250 increments each month while trying to keep Schmidt's going, even though I was barely tracking profits and losses. Our total household income was below $35,000, so we didn't have much, but it was enough.

I was at such an early stage of business with Schmidt's, but seeing my products on shelves in those tiny mom-and-pop shops was huge, and nothing was more gratifying than hearing from excited customers at markets. I was ready to jump into the year ahead with both feet, and that eagerness and persistence was about to take me further than I ever could have imagined. In order to rise to the challenge, I channeled an attitude I've often relied on: *say yes now, then figure out how*. The truth is, I still felt in over my head most of the time. I was collecting people's money but didn't have a business bank account or an accountant (I didn't even have the Square app yet, so I could only take cash or use an old-school manual credit card imprinter). I had a simple website but no online shop (aside from Etsy). I could go on with other examples of how my business was very DIY. I was figuring it all out on the go. Yet when an opportunity arose, I was determined not to let my lack of knowledge or experience stop me. So I'd say yes in the moment, then figure it out, one way or another. The more I did it, the easier it became, proving to myself how much I really could accomplish.

All this is to say that if you ever feel like an imposter, say yes to the opportunity in front of you. Say yes, even if you don't think you're ready or official enough. Chances are, you *can* figure it out (and/or you can find the people, resources, and tools to help you).

Make ends meet

At the part-time job I'd started the previous year, what had begun as a position heavy in grant writing (which was comfortable for me, as it involved little use of my voice) morphed into a communications role that was frankly beyond my expertise. And in this case, it wasn't one that I had any desire to say yes to. I wasn't feeling the job, especially with the new fundraising direction, and my employer knew it. So it wasn't a total surprise when I was presented with a severance option. Before leaving, I made sure every employee in the small office had one last jar of deodorant to remember me by, and said goodbye.

I saw unemployment as an opportunity to go all in with Schmidt's. The customer feedback I'd received was overwhelmingly positive, which helped validate what I was doing. I was eager to see how all my efforts would pay off in the coming season at the markets. I still needed some kind of supplemental income, but this time I was only interested in jobs that were somehow relevant to the DIY or maker lifestyle and reputation I was beginning to own. I had finally found my niche, and it allowed me to approach everything with a new sense of clarity and determination. I was committed.

The contact I'd made at the local ecommerce shop, Grow and Make, was a man named Will who was selling a few of my products online. I reached out and told him I was available for employment; was he hiring? He wrote back and to my surprise said yes. He'd been thinking about bringing someone on to help him create and expand the DIY kits the company sold. It was a perfect opportunity: I could work from home, be creative, and continue expanding my making expertise. I agreed immediately. Since the hours were few and the pay was low, I also enrolled in unemployment and used food stamps to make ends meet. I knew money would be tight, but our family did have the security of Chris's job, and we were all committed to seeing where my little business might go.

Since Will knew about my experience in the maker realm and was selling my Schmidt's creations on his site with success, one of my first assignments was to create lotion-making kits. This was fun. Besides, I'd already done the heavy lifting by perfecting my own lotion recipe. I sourced and packaged the raw materials that went into the lotion recipe, wrote up and designed instructions for the customer, and procured the right packaging to present the kits. Sometimes we even filmed step-by-step videos in his kitchen (with me strategically avoiding any on-camera speaking obligations, of course). Will gave me a target profit margin for each project, and I'd jump in. It was an excellent opportunity for research and learning. Over time, I created kits for making lip balm, soap, hot sauce, and candles, and for growing herbs.

In the meantime, I also reached out to The One Stop Sustainability Shop and picked up a few hours managing the register. It was a basic, low-paying retail job, but I loved the opportunity to see customers interact with my own products on the shelf, and it was another opportunity to learn about this niche market and what people were looking for when it came to natural products. Later, I ended up proposing a business collaboration where the Grow and Make DIY kits could be stored, assembled, and sold at The One Stop Sustainability Shop. It felt like all of my endeavors were in sync, and all of them fed my new passion. Anything I earned was essentially the seed money for Schmidt's.

When spring came, I went to farmers market upon farmers market, street festival after street festival, craft show after craft show, each time carefully setting up my booth with my handmade, hand-labeled lotions, deodorants, shampoo bars, and conditioner sprays. Some markets were very poorly attended, and I'd stand there all day, alone in the rain. There were plenty of moments of extreme self-doubt on those days, leaving me the time and space to question every decision I'd made. On occasion I'd be surrounded by disgruntled booth neighbors who had been selling their wares for years and were clearly burnt out. They'd make rude comments about customers or blame the hosts for a low turnout. I could tell their products were as tired as they were, like jars of jam that had absolutely no unexpected qualities, or hand-poured candles that were pretty enough but indistinguishable from others. Items with no personality or unique features faded quickly into the background, and if the maker exuded negative energy, that only made it worse. I knew my "brand" (if you could even call it that yet) wasn't particularly sophisticated, but I had a big Schmidt's banner printed and took care to arrange my products to showcase my simple logo and singular scents. Perhaps more crucially, I talked enthusiastically to anybody who walked by and looked curious about my booth. Still, it was hard not to wonder if this was all a big waste of time. *Was I going to just end up like the disgruntled neighbors? Could I break free from the market scene when the time was right?*

Ultimately, my confidence in my product kept me going. I continued to show up at weekend markets and collect customer feedback. Of all the products I was selling, the deodorant continued to elicit the most response. At markets that were better attended, people who I'd sold deodorant to weeks before would return with heartfelt, emotional testimonials saying the product had changed their life. I was awed. One woman told me how she was so self-conscious about her body odor that it was impacting her social life; she had found herself staying home because she worried about how she smelled. Every deodorant she'd tried either made her break out or smell even worse. Schmidt's, she said, actually worked. With tears in her eyes, she told me she felt liberated.

Others emailed me directly or left comments on social media. "Bought some of your deodorant at the Alberta Street Fair while I was vacationing in Portland," one wrote. "I love it! I wish it was sold in Texas, but will gladly pay shipping to keep using it. Winner!!"

Another wrote: "I seriously LOVE your deodorant . . . I have been searching for a natural deodorant that actually works and I didn't think one existed . . . until I found yours! I run, hike, bike, yoga . . . and NO stink. None! Wow!"

Whenever I could, I'd ask happy customers if I could share their comments on social media. Often these posts generated even more support and attention, helping to create a connection between my online and real-life communities.

This kind of feedback became commonplace. Once, a man walked up to me and asked for a handshake. I laughed and extended my hand, asking why. "Because one day you'll be famous for making a natural deodorant that actually works!" he said. Each time I received comments like this, I was moved. I'd known I wasn't the only one dissatisfied with existing natural deodorant options, but I never would have predicted that the home-brewed formula that worked so well for me would also work so well for others. Thanks to my customers, I began to see there was a huge gap in the market—one I might be able to fill. Soon, I'd learn that capitalizing on that opportunity would require me to grow into more roles than I ever expected: salesperson, marketing expert, operations manager, product developer, and CEO—a position I found myself naturally thrust into as the sole driver and decision-maker behind the business. Producing more deodorant for more people wouldn't simply be a logistical feat; it would push me to become a leader in ways I never imagined.

Know when to take feedback seriously
YOUR EARLY CUSTOMERS ARE YOUR FOCUS GROUPS

Note repetition. If a comment or request comes up again and again, it's worth seriously considering. Initially I made straightforward adjustments that I knew would please most customers and improve the product without too much effort. When customers repeatedly said they didn't like getting deodorant under their nails when applying it, for example, I started researching solutions.

But don't rush it. Customers will also offer suggestions you know you won't take, or ones that require a bigger investment of your time, creativity, and money. Keep track of it all and be patient. Many customers asked about a traditional stick version of the deodorant, which I knew would be a big challenge, involving a reformulation of my recipe, along with new containers, labels, and so on. I listened but also had to be realistic about what it might take to offer this option (eventually, it became a reality).

Customers challenged me, too. Farmers market attendees in Portland were especially informed and knowledgeable when it came to natural options, and were also sensitive to the overuse of the word "natural" and the fact that some brands "greenwashed," or presented themselves as all-natural or environmentally friendly when they really weren't. (All this made

Portland a great place to formulate.) At the booth, customers studied the ingredients lists closely. It wasn't uncommon for someone to ask, "Where did you source your baking soda?" or "What refining process did your shea butter go through?" I could speak about these things on a surface level but realized I needed to be prepared with a deeper knowledge of what I was talking about. I began to research and study up on my ingredients to make sure there was nothing I was overlooking. Conversations like these also helped me recognize the importance of my supply chain, so I could speak to where each ingredient came from. And the more I knew, the better I could confidently market myself by being able to talk about how I was committed to quality ingredients and how I was closely aligned with the farmers and suppliers I partnered with.

One day an email came in from a woman who said her sister had given her a jar of Schmidt's, which she loved. She added: "I understand that unless organic, cornstarch is generally made from genetically modified corn. Is the cornstarch you use GMO free? If not, do you have plans to offer a GMO-free deodorant in the future?" The GMO comment came up a few other times, and I listened. The following year, I began phasing out cornstarch in favor of arrowroot, which was quickly adaptable into my formula and had the added benefit of being completely odorless.

Another person emailed to say that shortly after she started using Schmidt's deodorant, she had developed a rash. I wrote back quickly, thanking her for the message and letting her know that it was the first I'd heard about the issue. From conversations with customers at markets and from my continued exploration and research, I was learning that some people believed their skin might be extra sensitive to baking soda or essential oils. Others preferred personal care products that weren't scented. While my cedarwood scent had been a hit so far, I could see the benefit of adding a fragrance-free option, which I had been offering as a lotion and knew might appeal to this audience. When the email came in, I was already in the process of preparing labels for a fragrance-free deodorant, and I told my customer it was coming soon, and that I'd give her one for free. She took me up on the offer and a few weeks later, I followed up to ask how it was working out for her. Her rash was gone, she said, and she loved the new version.

Early customer feedback allowed me to perfect my formula, determine future scents, and recognize where I was making the most impact. Most importantly, customers gave me validation that my product worked astonishingly well, and they spread the word. That boosted my confidence and my sales, and drove my growing commitment to my business. It's tempting at your first market—or in your first year—to fixate on the number of products sold. Because I wasn't dependent solely on Schmidt's for income, I was able to worry less about selling units and more about customer interactions, which were essential for improving my product and building community.

When opportunity knocks, open the door

One weekend in the summer of 2011, I noticed a woman walk by my booth a couple times, sort of sizing me up. When she finally approached, she introduced herself as Jasper, a manager at a local spa. She said she'd tried my lotions and was impressed by them, and she wondered if I'd consider a private label with her spa, Zenana. I instantly recognized the name

(I'd been there for a massage); it was a beautiful space with an amazing reputation. Jasper explained that the woman who was currently supplying their massage lotion was moving on, and they needed a replacement. I was stunned she was talking to *me* about this. *Can I really do this?* Without knowing with certainty that I could pull it off, I told her yes, I was interested.

On Monday, I emailed Zenana, saying I'd met Jasper and was eager to work together. "My lotion is made with all-natural ingredients and is available in a variety of scents or fragrance free. I would also be open to producing any custom scents that might suit your preferences," I wrote, adding, "I am happy to bring in samples and would love the opportunity to discuss further."

I knew it would be a huge challenge to create a formula that provided the perfect texture and glide for massage—very different from the lotion I was already making—and would be required in a much higher quantity. Most spas simply use oil, but Zenana was known for its lotion, which was apparently very popular with customers. This opportunity was a huge honor, and a chance to earn money and credibility while I continued testing and strengthening my new skills. I knew I'd figure it out. Zenana got back to me and said the challenge was mine.

One of the first things I did was email the woman who'd previously been making lotion for the spa. I figured she could help me with the formula and provide a little guidance. While I waited for a response, I started formulating, not wanting to waste any time. Online, I could see the ingredients listed in the spa's current lotion, which I was to draw inspiration from. However, I had no idea what amount of each ingredient to use, or how to get the texture and consistency just right in the heating and cooling process, as I'd done for my own products. Once again, there were so many factors: the ratio and sourcing of ingredients, the mixing process and length of time, and the room temperature at the time the product was made. My initial batches were all over the place—too watery, too greasy, too waxy, too thick, too thin.

When I still hadn't heard from the woman who had created the previous version, I asked Zenana for her number and called. On the phone, she was friendly, but politely told me that she was not open to disclosing any insight into her process or any information about ingredient ratios. She said she'd worked for months to perfect the blend and was not comfortable giving it away.

That made me sweat. Zenana wasn't paying me to figure this out; all the research and time invested was on me. What motivated me was knowing that if I nailed the lotion, I might have access to a steady stream of income from Zenana and I'd build my reputation as a maker of natural products. If I landed this project, I could use it to get others. And once I talked with the other supplier, even though she didn't help me get any closer to finishing the formula, I realized that once I *did* figure it out, I could keep it proprietary and reuse or sell it down the line.

Making compromises and difficult decisions is an ongoing part of being self-employed, no matter your field. It's a huge risk to work for free. You hope it pays off later—in more money, work, connections, and so on—but you can't predict the outcome in advance. Looking back, I'd tell my former self to charge for her time or propose a project budget, and to ask for more support from Zenana so that formulating wasn't just a shot in the dark.

After the phone call, I got back to work, all the more determined to crack the lotion code. I took sample after sample to Zenana so they could test my formula and offer feedback. I was getting closer. One night when Oliver was asleep and Chris was out at band practice, I was transferring a big bucket of lotion to a countertop in the kitchen when I dropped it. It spilled all over—across the counter, down into the cabinets, all over the floor. I called Chris. "It's everywhere!" I said, close to tears. He tried to soothe me and told me it would be okay. As determined as I was, spending so much time alone formulating was catching up to me, and I hadn't realized how stressed I was. It took every rag in the house to sop up the mess, which I piled on top of a mound of Oliver's dirty laundry and resolved to deal with in the morning. I was done for the night.

After a few more weeks of experimentation, I emailed Zenana with an update. Though they'd been patient, I felt the pressure to get them the formula they needed. "Let me first say that I enjoy a challenge, and this has been one!" I wrote, trying to remain optimistic. "Please know that I am determined and working diligently to develop a product as close in character to your current product as possible."

Finally, after over a month of formulating, I delivered a massage lotion that Zenana loved. The glide was perfect (oily enough to work with but not greasy), the consistency was there (not too thick or thin), and the scents were perfectly balanced (customers could choose from a spa signature blend, lavender, citrus, fragrance free, or a woody option). I was now the sole supplier of lotion for the spa. I was thrilled. I bought a hot plate and pot big enough to make a gallon at a time. Then I'd go through the process five times until I filled a five-gallon bucket. I'd repeat the whole process until I had five gallons of each scent. At least once a week, I'd load up the car with the buckets of lotion, strap Oliver into his car seat, and together we'd go deliver the lotion. Before long, Zenana customers were asking to purchase the lotion, so Zenana requested that I produce it in bottles in addition to the bulk. I worked with my designer, Rick, to create co-branded labels that included both the Zenana and Schmidt's names. This was an opportunity for exposure, and I was going to make sure people knew Schmidt's was behind the product they loved.

Then came more and more product ideas. Zenana loved having their name on the products and the fact that I was so willing to create anything they asked of me. Each time I'd say yes, then figure it out. There were hand/nail treatments, salt scrubs, lip scrubs, glitter "pixie" lotion, foot cream, and more.

To this day I have no idea whether I was earning a profit on the Zenana products. I didn't maintain proper balance sheets, and all the costs just got rolled into my other Schmidt's costs (which at the time were coming out of my and Chris's shared checking account and credit card, with no separation of personal and business expenses). I was learning heaps, forming connections, and building up my experience and credit as a local business. In retrospect, I recognize that while the gamble I took with Zenana ultimately became a big stepping-stone for me, I was lucky the effort didn't have negative financial consequences. Saying yes to a risky—and possibly costly—opportunity like this is a personal choice that every maker has to decide for themselves, given the circumstances. While my experience with Zenana was positive, my advice is to crunch the numbers in advance, keep track of your time, and be sure you're paid fairly.

Bookkeeping Basics
WHAT I WISH I KNEW WHEN I WAS FIRST STARTING OUT

Keep separate accounts. It's a best practice to keep all business expenses and income separate from your personal accounts to have "clean" books from the get-go. When you're starting out, this can mean a business bank account and maybe a credit card. Clean books are critical later if you're looking for investors, partners, or an eventual acquisition.

Run reports, or make them. Track income and expenses in your own spreadsheet or invest in a product like QuickBooks (which later allowed me to create balance sheets and profit and loss sheets, and do payroll and invoicing).

Determine what type of business you are. Different business types, such as sole proprietorship, LLC, S-Corp, and so on, have different tax implications and may cost money to set up. It's worth consulting with a lawyer or accountant for help.

Consider how and when you'll pay yourself. When you're first starting out, you may not be able to "pay" yourself from your profits. If you do pull money from the business, record it. Once you're profitable, you can determine standard owner draws on a scheduled basis and/or set up payroll, which an accountant can help with.

Don't forget estimated taxes. Even if you think you're not making much money, Uncle Sam will want a chunk of it. Track income and expenses so you can set aside money for estimated taxes as you go and avoid a surprise at tax time. This is another reason to hire a bookkeeper or accountant from the beginning.

Establish a pricing strategy

One day while I was standing at my Schmidt's booth at a market, the owner of a local mom-and-pop shop approached me and said, "We have people coming into our store asking for a local product called Schmidt's. Is that you? Do you have a line sheet?" I didn't have any idea what a line sheet was, but it was exciting to hear that people were looking for my product, and if this shop owner was proposing some sort of partnership, I wanted in. "You know, I don't have one here today, but if you give me your contact information I can follow up by email," I said.

Later, when I googled "line sheet," I realized it was simply an information sheet (also known as a wholesale sheet) listing my products and their wholesale prices, so that retailers could learn about them and consider stocking them in their stores. The other local shops had never asked for it because they sold Schmidt's on consignment. Once I started realizing there was another way, I began phasing out the consignment model. It had been a great entry point, but it was much more convenient for the store than for me. Smaller shops didn't have the money to pay for my product up front and didn't want to take the risk of paying for it and stocking it, only to have it sit on shelves without selling. But on my end, it was a pain to keep track of the inventory floating around out there and then just wait for the money to come in. As my confidence and know-how grew, I recognized how much easier it was to do wholesale.

First, however, I needed to create a line sheet, and in order to sell Schmidt's in this way, I'd also need barcodes (also known as universal product codes, or UPCs). Back to Google I went, where I found out that barcodes were pretty expensive. They had to be obtained through a global system called GS1, which required filling out a form and paying an initial setup fee of $250, plus the cost of the barcodes, and then waiting. But there was a workaround: instead of buying new barcodes, I could buy "recycled" ones that had previously been used by products that had since been retired, and these were much cheaper. The recycled ones were only thirty-five dollars a pop, and I could get them instantly. The only catch to buying the recycled codes was that they couldn't be used for products placed in large chain stores like Target. *Ha, that's no problem*, I said to myself, and bought the recycled, cheaper barcodes without a second thought.

Get retail ready
WHAT TO DO BEFORE YOU HIT SHELVES

Know your prices. Get help determining your wholesale price. Mine was approximately 40 to 50 percent of the retail price of the product (and still a healthy percent above COGS and other business costs to ensure a profit).

Set a minimum required order. It protects your time and encourages retailers to place bigger orders. As I learned later, large retailers often request a "free fill," or an opening order provided to them at no charge so they can test out your product—a policy that's typically non-negotiable. This means you're basically giving away free product, so it helps to be confident your product will do well at the store.

Make sure your labels are up to snuff. Unlike at a farmers market, at the store you won't be there to talk with customers. Make sure your labels are legally compliant, have barcodes, and offer enough information without looking cluttered. I recommend working with a designer who's familiar with label design and legal requirements.

Research insurance. Requirements can differ by industry and state. For a CPG product like mine, many retailers require liability insurance before stocking. You can check out local or independent options that specialize in products like yours, or consider working with an attorney. Heads-up that the forms can be tedious and no fun to fill out, but are just something you have to do.

Identify expiration dates and shelf stability. Research industry best practices on how to make legally sound calculations. Initially I determined expiration dates based on the ingredient with the shortest shelf life. Later, when I had lab tests done in order to sell in the EU, those calculations were verified.

Now I had my first line sheet (a more sophisticated version with pictures came soon after): a simple Word doc listing my products, their barcodes and brief descriptions, and what I thought was a fair wholesale price. My math was based on the little Google research I had done on pricing, which advised setting a wholesale price that is approximately half of your retail price. As time went on, I learned to calculate my COGS. This number changed over time, decreasing when I began buying in bulk and negotiating better deals on ingredients, and falling further in later years when I had automated machines for labeling and filling. Eventually I learned that for a product in the "consumables" category like mine (products that are "used up" and purchased recurrently), a healthy pricing structure is generally understood as one in which your retail price is roughly four to five times your COGS and your wholesale price is roughly two to three times your COGS (though this varies *significantly* across industries, retailers, and brands; those operating in tight margin industries, for instance, might have a structure that looks much different). I had become friendly with Polly, the owner of Local Goods, and consulted with her on how she thought I should price. Once I finalized prices, I emailed the line sheet to the woman I'd met at the farmers market, and not long after, I had my first wholesale account.

It wasn't always easy to say yes to a new opportunity without knowing with certainty that I could pull it off. But entrepreneurship requires taking risks, and I recognized the cost of saying no: I'd miss out on big chances to grow. Taking leaps of faith was necessary the entire time I grew Schmidt's, and the stakes only got higher. In the beginning, I operated based on guidance from my intuition, my customers, and my community. Later, I sought out expertise and deeper information by bringing on specialized consultants and conducting market research analysis. As the business became more sophisticated, so did I—but even when I was armed with more data and information, I needed to be comfortable taking chances and making hard decisions.

Have some fun doing it

As 2011 rolled on, I introduced my shampoo bars, conditioner spray, and sunscreen. I became a regular at one market in particular, attending almost every Sunday, and the organizers asked if I wanted to write an article in their weekly newsletter. "Yes!" I said, and wrote about the "no poo" method, where people wash their hair much less frequently and skip traditional shampoo and conditioner products in favor of more natural options, like baking soda with a vinegar rinse. It was trendy at the time, and I was positioning myself as knowledgeable about the latest in DIY body care. I used the article as an opportunity to say that when you *do* use shampoo, try Schmidt's shampoo bars—giving my own product a little plug. I continued to share product updates and other DIY recipes on Facebook, where folks I'd met at farmers markets (and even random strangers) were increasingly following me and trusting me as a knowledgeable resource.

As the holiday season approached, I added bath salts to my lineup, recognizing that it was a more "giftable" item to some people than, say, a jar of deodorant. At the time, I figured, the more products, the better. Still, since deodorant had been the trickiest to formulate, and had remained the most unique item—not to mention one I got the most enthusiastic responses to—it was always the first thing I talked about when someone approached my booth. And it was far and away my favorite, too.

In December, I hosted my very own makers market, the Winter Solstice Sundown. On a slim budget, I rented the local VFW hall for an evening, with a cash bar for a festive mood. A friend designed a poster, advertising the event as "sponsored by Schmidt's." I had attended dozens of fairs and markets at this point, and I wanted a chance to do it my way. Schmidt's was becoming more well known around the city, and I was eager to continue to grow my reputation. Chris helped me choose local musicians to play throughout the event, and

I solicited applications for vendors. My goal was to display a variety of products, but not wanting to discriminate, I essentially accepted applicants on a first-come, first-served basis. The event filled up fast, and I used every inch of the space at the venue. In addition to the musicians, I invited a local Girl Scout troop to sing Christmas carols. We had a huge turnout, and everything went off without a hitch (well, there was one angry vendor who complained one of the "screeching" musicians had given her a headache and demanded her registration fee be refunded). I didn't make any money on the event, but I loved the opportunity to experience firsthand how a market is planned and executed, and it was so gratifying to be the host.

By the end of 2011, I felt like I was on fire with my business. All my hard work to get into as many markets as possible, offer products at local shops, co-brand my work for Zenana, and expand my expertise and my community seemed to be paying off. I felt more confident than ever, and I had a vision for taking Schmidt's further. For the first time in my life, I felt completely devoted to and passionate about my work. It all began when the excitement and pride I felt at having finally found "my thing" led me to want to share it with the world. I discovered that the community built in the process was rewarding beyond measure. Only by connecting with those around me was I able to hone my formula, cultivate an early following, and get my products to the next level. ∎

What to make of it

 Challenge yourself.

Rise to the occasion, take chances, and seize opportunities for growth. This doesn't mean saying yes to everything, or working for free, or doing something you're uncomfortable with. But do have faith you can figure out *how*, even if it takes a while, even if you need to ask for help.

 Leave room to adapt and evolve.

Some people launch with a hard-core business plan and immediately invest in all the infrastructure they think they will need. As an entrepreneur, your direction will likely deviate as you begin hearing from your customers and identifying your strengths, as well as your limits. Listening to my customers offered an organic path toward growth and improvement—one I couldn't have devised myself in a formal business plan.

 Your community is your launchpad.

Being present and attentive with customers, market orga-nizers, fellow makers, local shop owners, and social media followers is how Schmidt's initially took off. My community supported me with feedback and opportunities, which turned into my foundation for growth.

Exceptional

Claim your corner of the market + distinguish your brand

CHAPTER 4

Zero in to scale up.

Refine your offerings to capitalize on your niche.

A round the same time that I was approached by Zenana, I'd enrolled in a free local course called "Foundations of Business" in an effort to support my fledgling business. It was offered by Mercy Corps NW, an NGO headquartered in Portland, and I signed up when I learned that attendees got the opportunity to qualify for a small business loan. I didn't really need a class—I did have a business degree, after all—but the chance to land a small sum of money to invest into Schmidt's was appealing. I could use it for supplies, or maybe to update my website or try advertising for the first time. I never did get the loan, but I learned a thing or two.

One night in class, I stood in front of a room of fellow small business owners, smiled nervously, and took a deep breath. It was my turn to deliver an elevator pitch for my business. While I had grown completely comfortable talking with customers at a farmers market booth or walking into a grocery store and introducing myself, addressing a room full of people, all eyes on me, made me cringe. I knew my voice condition would make me sound even more nervous than I was. The best I could do was avoid words I knew might trip me up and make the best of it. My heart thundered in my chest. I breathed in and delivered my pitch. It went something like this:

> *Schmidt's is a beauty product line made locally here in Portland, and I am the proud sole proprietor of the business. Schmidt's was inspired by a desire to offer safe, healthy alternatives to big-brand commercial products. Most of my products are packaged in reusable glass jars and are made with only natural, non-synthetic ingredients. Schmidt's deodorant and lotion are favorites among customers, along with shampoo bars, conditioner sprays, and a mineral protection sunscreen.*

Around town, I'd found that emphasizing the fact that I was a one-woman show, based locally and using all-natural ingredients, was effective. Local shops liked the sound of what I was doing, and friends and acquaintances were impressed. Plus, there was a huge opportunity in the market for a natural deodorant that performed well. I was growing increasingly ambitious about my company's potential.

But delivering my pitch that night, I suddenly got the sinking feeling it might have its shortcomings. One at a time, my classmates raised their hands and asked questions like, "But what *really* makes these products different?" and "Why are they special?" We were all meant to push one another to improve our pitches so that our "unique value propositions" were clear and memorable. But I found myself struggling to offer compelling answers with confidence.

What *was* special about Schmidt's? What would it take to get to the next level? When I considered my classmates' questions, I began to wonder.

Stake your claim

During another session of the business course, the instructor asked all of us to stand up, then told all but one or two to sit back down. Those still standing represented the tiny percentage of business ideas that would succeed, she said. To increase your chances of success, she told us, you need to offer a product that's unique compared to what's already on the market. This was obvious, of course, but the lesson resounded for me in a new way. I had a lightbulb moment where I understood I could accomplish far more by focusing on just one product and doing it right. Specializing in deodorant would differentiate me from other personal care brands trying to do it all.

The idea percolated in the back of my mind for months. After taking the course in 2011, I continued to sell my whole line of products. But when I talked about my deodorant—and when my customers talked about it, for that matter—it was obvious there was a singular, unmatched excitement. As I went through my inbox and looked at the Schmidt's Facebook page, I found testimonial after testimonial about it. Many said they'd switched from more popular natural brands, which to me was the most validating of any of the feedback. I never dreamed I'd be competing with the big names in deodorant.

At farmers markets and beyond, I was earning a reputation as the "Deodorant Girl" or "Pit Queen." It definitely wasn't something I'd ever imagined for myself, but the more I embraced it, the more passionate and possessive I became. When I pitched retailers, I always led with deodorant, saying it was my bestseller. Focusing on the thing I did best, instead of running through my whole product line, made my pitch flow more naturally.

One of my earliest goals had been to land a wholesale account at a local food co-op. Portland had many popular ones, and I knew getting my product on their shelves would legitimize the brand. Here's a pitch I sent to a local co-op late in 2011, in which I introduced Schmidt's as a brand:

Schmidt's is a local producer of all-natural body care products for women and men. Our deodorant is our top-selling product. We consistently hear positive feedback from customers who tell us Schmidt's deodorant keeps them dry and free of odor, even after extended periods of physical activity. Customers regularly report that Schmidt's is the only natural deodorant that works for them. Our formula allows for the body's natural process of perspiring, while effectively absorbing wetness and neutralizing odor. A combination of all-natural ingredients moisturizes and soothes the sensitive underarm area; the subtle fragrance of cocoa butter is complemented by a blend of essential oils for a light, natural scent.

It worked! I pitched another co-op, Alberta Street Co-op, toward the end of 2011, specifically highlighting my deodorant. When they accepted, I was over the moon.

"Are you sure you want to phase out *all* your other products?" Chris questioned as we sat at the kitchen table one night. To him, the idea sounded counterintuitive. Why would I want to sell fewer products instead of more? But I was convinced, and when he heard how sure I was about my new direction, soon he was, too. I knew I could offer something that wasn't on the market—not just a natural deodorant that worked, but one with interesting new scents and well-designed, contemporary packaging. To me, it was clear that if I devoted all my energy to my bestseller, nothing could stop me. If starting at the farmers market could lead me to the local co-op, why shouldn't the next step be the local grocery store, then grocery chains, and beyond? Choosing to focus solely on deodorant was a monumental moment for me—suddenly my vision for my business was clear. Despite pushback from friends and family who thought I was limiting myself, by the start of 2012, I assumed my new identity as the creator of Schmidt's Deodorant.

Setting your own goals
MAKE PROGRESS ON YOUR OWN TERMS

Take small steps. You don't have to create a long list of finite goals; instead, I always preferred to focus on moving ahead incrementally. Each new business development is a step forward, and each time you take one step, you can identify the next one, and then the next.

Maintain a big vision. Your small steps should lead you toward it. My big vision was for my product to be widely available and reach as many people as possible. That idea became my North Star and informed which small steps to take.

Look the part

The volume of competition I was up against became real when an Alberta Street Co-op employee brought me to the back of the store to show me the number of samples they received every day from small business owners like me.

Some were beautiful, professionally packaged lotions, lip balms, and other natural body care products with special symbols and certifications on the labels—yet none had won a spot on the co-op's shelves. Mine had been chosen, she said, because she loved the cedarwood scent and the fact that the product was made locally. Still, seeing those rejected samples, my competitive spirit grew even more fierce. How could I make sure my deodorant would stand out above the rest?

I began planning a rebrand of Schmidt's, with new packaging and additional scents. My cedarwood and fragrance-free deodorants had taken me far, but customers were asking for a floral scent, presenting me with an opportunity to get creative. As I prepared to rebrand, I decided to change my cedarwood offering to Cedarwood + Juniper, and to introduce a new scent, Ylang-Ylang + Calendula.

When I developed scents, I didn't do any heavy-duty research but instead went with my intuition. I trusted my own tastes and preferences. And at this point I'd developed a good sense of who my customers were and what they'd find appealing.

Ylang-Ylang + Calendula was a sweet, subtle scent with floral notes (it's still my all-time favorite). I loved how unusual the word "ylang-ylang" looked and sounded (pronounced "ee-lang ee-lang"), and the fact that the color and scent of the flower evoked tranquility and stress relief. I discovered that juniper oil was very strong and could quickly become overpowering, so it took time to balance it just right with the cedarwood, resulting in a warm, woody scent. Both combinations would appeal to any gender (I hoped), and were affordable for me to make, as their essential oils weren't at the upper end of the price spectrum. By this point, I'd learned a lot about the world of essential oils. Pricing ranged significantly depending on the abundance of a particular plant, the harvesting process, the ease of distillation, and the yield of distillation. For example, it takes fifty roses to produce a single drop of rose essential oil, which can drive the price up to $200 for five milliliters.

My designer friend Rick had done an amazing job with my initial logo and labels, and I loved his work (I still work with him to this day; he even created the illustrations for this book!). But as I planned to rebrand from Schmidt's Beauty to Schmidt's Deodorant, I saw value in getting a new, outside perspective. In the beginning, my logo and packaging fit perfectly with the farmers market scene. They had a quaint, homestead look that gave a nod to the natural ingredients and made it clear they were small-batch products, which appealed to local and sustainably minded shoppers. But once I set my sights on growth, I realized my audience would not only be shopping at the markets but also in the aisles of grocery stores. My deodorant would need to "dress the part" for its new role as a disrupter on shelves, distinguishing itself as a modern, new brand. I noticed other natural deodorants at the time were packaged in bland, beige-y colors with stock photos of flowers in meadows. I wanted mine to be different, grab attention, and look irresistible.

I hired a local design firm in Portland, one of my first "official" business collaborations. I liked the work they'd done at some local restaurants and reached out, even though I didn't exactly have a budget for the project and couldn't afford much. When they pitched an extensive design package, I insisted I only needed a logo and three label designs, one for each scent. It was a small project for them, so I was grateful when they took me on as a client anyway.

In our first meeting, I did my best to articulate my ideas for the rebrand. For some reason I was convinced I should go in a "scientific" direction for the logo. I thought it could communicate a modern approach to the formula while still looking approachable. I wanted to use bright colors—each scent would have its own—that worked together and popped on shelves. I wanted to be adventurous. I wanted to grab attention, and I wanted the design to say "premium" so that my deodorant looked beautiful and luxurious from store shelves to bathroom vanities.

Build an inspired visual identity
BE SURE YOUR BRAND STANDS OUT

Go professional. A strong visual brand identity is so important. It's the first thing customers see, and everyone's a critic. The field of branding requires highly developed skills, so find designers you trust. This was the first aspect of my business that I handed over, and the investment paid off.

Take risks. When it comes to your look, be willing to do the opposite of what everyone else is doing. Go into your dream retailer, scope out the competition, and do whatever you can to avoid looking like them. If they go bland, you go full of life. If they go dark, you go light. If they make certain claims on their packaging, you focus on differentiating yours. I have seen brands succeed through imitation, but to me this approach can only take you so far.

Remember, you're creating a visual world. The colors, fonts, and illustration styles must work in a variety of contexts: in print (on the labels, but also in things like pitch decks), online (in social media and on your website), and at a larger scale (retail banners, etc.). Make design guidelines to establish consistency.

The designers listened closely, and it didn't take long before they presented a version I loved. The end result was modern, colorful packaging that celebrated each unique scent. For Cedarwood + Juniper, we chose a rich brick red color, while Ylang-Ylang + Calendula was a golden yellow, and Fragrance Free was a deep sky blue. The colors worked well on their own and sitting next to each other as a family. Later, when I introduced new scents, the design team would regularly tweak all the colors slightly so they continued to work in harmony. The labels were not only beautiful; the design firm made sure to use required minimum font sizes and necessary content, like the city, state, and zip code of manufacture. The logo was my favorite part. The custom serif font had a subtle scientific influence, reminiscent of the famous NASA logo, and the result was an unexpected, contemporary logo that was unlike anything else in the natural body care space.

Another step of the rebrand process was finding the perfect container. I'd been selling the deodorant first in Mason jars and then in small, round aluminum tins, but the product didn't sit vertically on shelves, so people couldn't see the logo. My friend Brad, a local maker of beeswax lip balm, had been making wooden stands that propped up the tins, which I'd deliver to each new retailer, but the system wasn't sustainable. I briefly considered screen printing the new labels on white plastic jars but didn't like the mockups at all—they looked cheap, and I quickly realized I wanted to stick with glass for the jars. Instead of going back to small Mason jars, I found glass jars that were similar in size that could be purchased online in bulk, saving me money while also presenting the more sophisticated, sustainable look I was after. This helped me achieve my ultimate goal of having a product that would stand out (and beg for photography) on a bathroom vanity. Plus, you could see the product on the shelf through the glass jar without having to open the lid. For now, I'd have to continue to hand-label the jars, but to achieve the effect I wanted, it was worth it.

Once the redesign was complete, I hired a local photographer to take a bunch of product photos that I could use on social media and my website, in pitches to retailers, and in any other way that might be useful down the road. When I finally introduced the new look to customers, the feedback was immediately and overwhelmingly positive. Schmidt's instantly looked like a serious contender in the deodorant aisle. The rebrand helped attract the attention of boutiques, online shops, and local spas, in addition to the co-ops and small shops I'd started in. I reached out to many of the stores that had previously ignored or rejected me, and many were suddenly extremely interested, thanks to the standout new packaging. And not long after, doors began opening for exciting opportunities at national retail locations.

Be resilient with retailers and buyers

After nearly two years in business, Schmidt's had become a regular fixture at markets across Portland (I'm talking every street fair, festival, farmers market, and craft show at churches, schools, and parks year-round), and while I recognized the biggest opportunity for growth was in retail accounts, I still gained immense value from showing up at my weekend markets and fairs. Getting first-hand feedback from customers motivated me more than anything else. Their enthusiasm fueled me. While the markets weren't the biggest money-maker, or even the best way to get exposure (because you start to see the same faces over and over), they were a huge boost to my confidence, happiness, and motivation. Today, when entrepreneurs tell me they do most of their business online, I always encourage them to take every opportunity they can to communicate with their customers, even though they aren't face to face. Be active in the comments, ask for feedback, send newsletters, and encourage responses. Be transparent and share the feedback you're getting (and how you're implementing it) with your audience. Customers are your focus groups, and not only do they have a lot to teach you, but they can support and encourage you in infinite other ways.

An initial benefit of the markets was meeting local shop owners who came to the booth interested in Schmidt's. But once I really owned the idea of wholesale and had my newly rebranded product, I decided I wasn't going to wait around for stores to approach me. I began investing more time in courting retailers, either by stopping by the store (often with Oliver on my hip) or pitching by email. I mailed samples of the deodorant to all the retailers in the area, and personally followed up to see what people thought.

For each account I landed, I'd add the store to a locator on my website so visitors could easily find where to buy Schmidt's. The store locator started as a simple list of store names, and later Chris designed an interactive map with a little "S" flag to mark each location, and it was a thrill to watch the map (and eventually, the globe) literally fill up with S flags as we continued to land more and more accounts. I used existing accounts to appeal to new ones—for example, by telling a potential retail partner, "Schmidt's is already selling well at [such-and-such] store across town," to emphasize the brand's desirability. I was hustling to bring in accounts myself, but in time, I'd learn that I could work with broker teams to land more accounts in exchange for commission, and ultimately many of my biggest accounts were brought in this way.

I landed my first chain grocery store account, PCC Community Markets, by being extra tenacious. I initially met Wendy, a representative from the company, at a gift show in Seattle (the first out-of-town show I'd ever traveled to). Gift shows are targeted specifically toward retailers looking to open new wholesale accounts, and they're not open to the public. Generally you pay to have a booth, and there isn't much screening required to get in. Gift shows offered huge opportunities to land accounts, though as Schmidt's grew, I attended more trade shows than gift shows, as not everyone viewed deodorant as the most giftable item. (Eventually I introduced a gift set of deodorant jars packaged together to dispel this notion.) Similar to gift shows, trade shows are closed to the public and targeted specifically toward store buyers. No matter what kind of show it was, my goal was to convince buyers that my product would fly off their shelves. After an initial conversation with Wendy in Seattle, I got her business card and was quick to follow up first thing Monday morning.

"I've written up the attached order based on our conversation at the gift show," I said in my email (perhaps I was a little forward, but I was eager to get the ball rolling).

When Wendy didn't respond after a week, I wrote again and said, "I'm planning to ship your order this week if that works well for you. Can you please confirm the address where the opening order should be sent?"

Of course, I wasn't going to send off a batch of deodorants without Wendy's confirmation (and payment), but I was trying to get her attention. It worked. She responded immediately, writing, "NO! Please don't do that. I don't even have you set up as a vendor." But she promised to reach out again when she was ready for me. It was a bold move on my part. For a couple months, I didn't hear anything, but sure enough, she followed up, and we proceeded to set up the account.

At this stage, bigger grocery stores like this one wouldn't have just offered to put Schmidt's on shelves (though it did happen later on). I had to be much more persistent, sometimes following up repeatedly after an initial contact, just to remind store buyers that Schmidt's existed. Sometimes I'd include notes like, "Check out all the great feedback customers are sharing on this social media post," to keep the conversation alive. I also had to know when to be patient, because often I had to wait for enough customers to go in asking for Schmidt's before a store was convinced I was worth their investment. At times I encouraged customers to ask stores directly to carry Schmidt's, and I even filled out comment cards myself to get on their radar (a girl's gotta do what a girl's gotta do). I learned about category resets, the retail cycles that dictate when a store considers which new products to bring in for each category, and I started asking store employees when they would be updating their deodorant category so I'd know the right time of year to pitch. This information became crucial, especially when the accounts got bigger—I didn't want to miss a window that generally came only once a year.

Knowing when and how to talk with retailers—or specifically with buyers, the retail reps in charge of bringing in new products at a store—was a skill I had to develop. Once, as I pitched a big grocery store, I mentioned that my customers often told me they switched from Tom's of Maine to Schmidt's. "And how does that benefit us?" the buyer responded. I immediately realized my error; if current customers switched from one brand to another, that didn't result in any growth in sales for the store. They wouldn't see a gain. That taught me that it was much more effective to talk about how Schmidt's could attract *new* customers to their location. And, I'd mention that these new customers were willing to pay up to eight dollars for Schmidt's, more than they paid for competitors' products, thereby bringing in greater revenue to the store (this is called "trading up," which stores loved to hear about). With the Schmidt's social media accounts bustling with customer engagement, I'd be sure to mention that I'd advertise new retailers to my online followers and help direct traffic to them, too.

Pitch secrets

HOW TO TALK TO LOCAL RETAILERS + GET YOUR PRODUCT ON SHELVES

Know what you're up against. Retailers see *a lot* of product. Come in prepared to talk about how yours differs from what's on shelves and what type of sales performance they can expect.

Know your customer. Talk about who buys your product (ideally new customers for the store). Above all else, demonstrate what's in it for the retailer.

Never trash talk other brands. It's unprofessional. Focus on why your product is great without putting down the competition.

Bring everything in writing. I started out with a basic line sheet, which evolved into a line sheet with product pictures, which became a branded folder including the line sheet, a presentation about the company, and a press sheet (plus, samples).

Get personal. Relationships are everything. If you're meeting with a buyer who makes you nervous, learn something about them beforehand. Maybe you have something in common, like a hobby, home state, or other interest.

Say yes. Retailers want to know if you'll be game to collaborate with them. Determine the amount of product you can give away or discount as a marketing expense. When retailers asked if I could do buy-one-get-one promos, provide free product for an initial test run, or commit to multiple promotions throughout the year, I said yes. When my product was discounted, more customers tried it, which meant more money (and word of mouth) in the long run.

Determine your delivery standards and methods

In addition to my growing presence in local stores, I always had a steady flow of online orders, which I packed and shipped as quickly as I could. At first, I maintained my Etsy shop, then later I asked Chris to help me redesign my website to include a web shop. Occasionally big orders came through at random, but in general, transactions were pretty minimal; my social media audience was steadily growing, but I wasn't advertising yet. Since most of my customers were local at that time, they tended to buy my product at my booths or in stores.

Depending on the market, I was selling anywhere from ten to fifty jars of deodorant in a given day. With the uptick in retail accounts, though, I had to produce much more deodorant and get it to stores. For a while, I drove the jars around town and delivered them personally, often with Oliver (and his favorite stuffy, Bear) along for the ride. At first, without an order minimum, stores could request to stock, say, just a case of deodorant (six jars), and I'd provide their order. When they sold out or ran low, I'd get a new order request and return with a delivery. Soon I was spending one or two days a week driving all over town, delivering to my accounts. As I expanded my retail presence, this became unsustainable. I was wasting precious time and spending all my money on gas. Would it be smarter to ship the orders? I priced out the cost of different boxes and packaging options (I'd need to carefully protect the glass jars), plus shipping fees. My money would stretch the furthest using USPS flat rate boxes with plenty of packing peanuts to make sure the jars were secure. (After I once spent the better part of an afternoon chasing runaway peanuts and sweeping them up off the street, I was excited to find an eco-friendly, biodegradable option that would break down in water.)

I also implemented an order minimum: three cases. When I realized most orders were for three to six cases, I offered a deal for free shipping if you ordered eight, hoping to incentivize larger buys. This strategy helped increase my sales, but when a handful of small shops continued to request smaller orders (often with free shipping), I always made exceptions, not wanting to harm long-standing relationships.

The switch to shipping was a trade-off: instead of driving all around Portland delivering deodorant, I spent more time packing boxes and waiting in line at the post office. I also needed to find a way to store all those boxes and packing peanuts in our tiny house. I started to wonder if I'd soon need to hire help.

Meanwhile, I began spending my Saturday mornings as a volunteer intern at the Herb Shoppe, a local store where customers came to explore natural medicines and remedies. Surrounded by walls lined with tinctures, herbs, and tea blends, the shop was like a little paradise for me as well as a classroom. I figured spending a few hours a week there was a worthy investment of my time if I could expand my knowledge of natural goods and remedies and continue to immerse myself in the scene. It was important that I know about my target customer—it made my decision-making skills sharper. Plus, I have a genuine enthusiasm for herbs and natural remedies, and I learned so much that I could apply to my personal routine. When I went to the shop on Saturdays and the markets on Sundays, Chris was happy to have the time with Oliver and often helped by going on supply pickups.

Trust when it's time to go all in

By the end of 2012, my local retail accounts were emailing and calling to say my product was selling like crazy. I'd be mid-deodorant-making in the kitchen when I'd see the time and realize I had to rush to my shift at Grow and Make or the Herb Shoppe, or I'd get a call from the spa in need of a few new gallons of lotion. I simply didn't have time for it all. I was ready to quit the part-time gigs that had been helping fund my company. Chris and I knew how much we needed each month to survive (for rent, food, childcare, etc.) and between his job, some savings, the knowledge that my parents could likely help in a pinch, and the faith that my business would continue to grow, we felt secure enough financially for me to go all in on deodorant-making. Chris and I were a team. He often helped with Schmidt's tasks, but more importantly, his schedule allowed him to share household and childcare responsibilities equitably and to pick up the slack when I got busy. That was huge.

It wasn't always comfortable, but I was able to tolerate risk and uncertainty pretty well, and that helped me take a leap of faith. I was ready to put my whole self into Schmidt's. I knew if I invested all my time into my business, I could break beyond the limits of what I'd initially dreamt was possible.

One night in December, as the holidays approached, I had a dream that my mom and grandma attended a craft fair and came to my booth. My Grandma Norrie, who had recently passed away, said, "Wow, this looks really nice." Mom said, "Jaime knows what she's doing." Grandma laughed her little laugh and said, "Why, I know she does, Pam."

I woke up the next morning and wrote down my dream so I wouldn't forget. Though I wasn't entirely sure that I *did* know what I was doing, hearing them voice their faith in me—even in a dream—made me feel reassured that I was on the right path. ∎

What to make of it

 Define your niche, then claim it.

It's true what they say: you can't be everything to everyone. Identify your specific opportunity in the market and carve it out as your own. Culling your offerings doesn't necessarily mean you're scaling back; in fact, it can mean you're honing in.

 Go all in with your branding.

As soon as I knew the precise arena in which I was competing, it became easier to determine the way in which I wanted to stand out amongst competitors. Beautiful design was an obvious and important area for differentiation. We all judge books by their covers and products by their branding. Investing in professional design set up Schmidt's for success.

 Know your (other) audience.

Beyond customers, retailers were a critical audience for my brand. In order to grow, it was crucial for me to learn how to communicate with, appeal to, and work with retail partners. Smart brands are aware of the perception they have amongst all their partners, from retailers to ingredient suppliers to sales and packaging brokerages and beyond. Forming strong relationships with everyone you do business with is not just best practice, it is a necessity for smart growth.

CHAPTER 5

Mind your own business.

Don't get distracted by the competition; invest in what makes your product singular.

I n the early days of starting Schmidt's, I didn't pay *too* much attention to my competition. I knew most natural deodorants hadn't worked for me and that many brands seemed outdated. But instead of going far down the rabbit hole with research on my competitors, I focused on the quality of my product. Looking back, I believe those blinders helped get me ahead and kept me from getting intimidated or paralyzed by second-guessing myself. I easily could have been sidetracked or influenced by my competitors, distracted from my own intuitive sense of what was best for my product and business. For a time, ignorance was—if not bliss—very constructive.

Rise above

But once I saw the real potential of Schmidt's and had been exposed to that heap of rejected samples at Alberta Street Coop, I became very competitive. When even small competitors showed up on my radar, it was a challenge for me to ignore them. One began following everyone who followed Schmidt's on Twitter, including random connections like people I'd known from high school. Not cool, I thought—these were *my* people. Soon I was looking at social media accounts of every deodorant brand I could find, analyzing their product, branding, and followers. I couldn't help myself sometimes, and I'd spend late nights deep in stalker mode ("Facebook creeping," I would call it). I was losing sleep—and focus.

At farmers markets and craft fairs, I usually got to enjoy the relative comfort of being the only deodorant maker on the scene. When other natural beauty brands were in my midst, I liked to check them out, and they did the same with me. We were friendly, but we had our eye on one another. There was one local maker in Portland who was well known for her soaps and lotions—someone with a great reputation and pretty extensive retail distribution, too. We often made small talk, and I liked her, but when she mentioned to me that she had been working on a deodorant formula she hoped to launch, my palms began to sweat (my armpits stayed nice and dry, of course). I launched Schmidt's at a time when the natural deodorant trend wasn't very widespread, and I'd worked hard to establish myself as *the* deodorant maker in Portland. What would I do when competitors entered my space?

Unfortunately, I already had a few. Whenever I talked with customers about other deodorant brands they'd tried, there was one niche brand mentioned frequently. It was one of the more serious upstarts in the natural deodorant space. Like Schmidt's, this brand's deodorant came in a jar, and the formula was somewhat similar, leading customers to frequently compare the two. Sometimes someone would ask me directly, "How is your deodorant different from theirs?" To this, I'd often repeat things I'd heard from enthusiastic customers all the time: that Schmidt's scents were one of a kind and well balanced, for instance. I always smiled and kept it positive, even though I hated knowing I was competing with this other company.

Once, I signed up to attend a craft festival about an hour outside Portland. After arriving and setting up my booth, I was surprised to see another maker selling deodorant. Immediately my defenses went up. Was she aware of Schmidt's and trying to steal my thunder? She came over to my booth and introduced herself, commenting on how uncanny it was that we each made the same product. "Do you want to trade?" she asked, saying something about how we could check out each other's formulas. I politely declined. Even though it was awkward to say no, I was instinctively protective of my business. I also understood more than ever why the former lotion maker at Zenana didn't want to hand over her formula to me. When you work so hard to achieve something, there's a desire to protect it.

Another time, when Schmidt's was well established in the Pacific Northwest and on the West Coast and beginning to make its way east, I received an email from a customer on the East Coast. She said she'd been visiting a friend in California when she was introduced to Schmidt's, and she fell in love with the deodorant.

"I'd love to start making some deodorant here for all us stinky East Coasters," she wrote. "Would you be willing to give me a suggestion on where I could buy shea butter?"

The email had a sweet, friendly tone, but it struck me as odd, that instead of ordering Schmidt's online or asking when it would be available near her, she wanted to know about sourcing shea butter. I thanked her for reaching out and told her I had plans to make my product more widely available, without getting into the topic of shea butter suppliers. She wrote back that she understood, and the exchange ended there, on what felt like perfectly pleasant terms.

About a year later, I was on Instagram browsing the hashtag #naturaldeodorant when I found pictures of deodorant in the same jars as mine, with similar scents. I went to the company's profile and, after a little digging, discovered it was the same woman who had emailed me over a year before. It looked like she'd blatantly ripped off Schmidt's! It's flattering to be an inspiration, but sheesh, a little originality would have been nice.

Keeping it to yourself
IT'S OK TO SAY "THAT'S PROPRIETARY"

Formula and techniques. Chances are there are numerous processes, techniques, ingredients, "hacks," or approaches you use in your business that give you an edge. A few times I was asked, "What kind of mixers do you use?" or "How are you breaking up your butters?" I always politely declined to share details about my machinery and the process I'd worked so hard to perfect. It's okay not to share.

Raw material suppliers. If you're buying ingredients and supplies from sources you've developed relationships with—especially local or smaller businesses— you might keep that information private in order not to compromise your own supply.

Business partners. Working with designers and other collaborators can be a huge investment. Of course I wanted to be helpful to fellow makers, but if a potential competitive threat wanted a referral for a good designer, I didn't necessarily offer the information.

Specific pitch techniques. The way you communicate with retailers, influencers, bloggers, and buyers will likely become more nuanced over time. You'll learn what grabs attention and incentivizes people (for me, one example was using case studies of past successes in my pitch decks), but you don't need to broadcast these lessons to others.

Social media strategies. As you try different approaches, you'll learn which types of posts resonate most with your audience. With Schmidt's, people often asked Chris and me to share our recipe for success. If it was a competitor asking, we had to refrain; it'd taken time to understand what resonated with customers.

I encountered another fraught situation the very first time I hired help. Eventually, I was selling so much deodorant that I couldn't keep up with production. I needed assistance. It was an extremely informal affair: I simply asked a friend who had downtime if I could pay him an hourly rate to come help me make batches. He agreed, and a day or two later, he was at my house learning to make deodorant.

I provided handwritten instructions detailing what to add when, at what temperature, and so on. It was such a relief to have some help; I had been working ten to twelve-hour days to keep up with orders. He continued to pitch in for a few weeks until I hired someone more permanent.

Not long after, I opened Facebook one night and saw that his girlfriend was promoting *her* new deodorant company. I panicked. Had he given her my recipe? I called Chris over to my computer, totally freaking out. "Can you believe this?" I exclaimed. "What am I going to do?" He texted our friend;

apparently the couple had already split up. We never got to the bottom of exactly what happened, but we knew he was a great guy, and it was clear there was no bad intent on his part. Still, there was the issue of what to do about the new copycat brand, and she was also in Portland, which made it more annoying.

What more could I do? I felt powerless. It was the same way I felt when the East Coast deodorant brand popped up in my Instagram feed. Chris helped me calm down, stand back, and take a more level-headed look at the situation. Together we looked at the landscape of all our competitors' social media presences from a bird's-eye view. They were clearly less established than Schmidt's, with fewer followers and maybe less enthusiasm around the brand. I'd been sharing Schmidt's updates on Facebook for a few years, along with DIY recipes, photos, testimonials, and details about where people could buy Schmidt's in stores or find me at a local market. There was always a steady stream of people commenting about ingredients, asking questions, tagging their friends, and encouraging me. I also had a long email list of subscribers receiving my newsletters, in which I announced product updates, new retail locations, or upcoming events. I had an engaged community that was growing organically, which Chris helped me see was what I should be focusing my energy on.

I also tried to shift my perspective on the copycats. Even though I was frustrated, I had to admit copying was a form of flattery. Maybe friendly competition was a good thing. With more brands on the market, more people would be exposed to natural deodorant, and that could help lead customers to Schmidt's—especially since I knew I'd built a strong, solid reputation as the natural option that really worked.

Growing a small business is hard work, and it's all consuming. I was doing it because I *loved* it. I was passionate, I truly believed in my product, and I had a vision for it. But if a copycat was simply mimicking me to try to earn money, I doubted they'd have the drive and devotion it would require to really build something. Copying can only take you so far.

Most of all, spotting these brands got me thinking about how to strengthen my own position in the market. I grew more motivated to think bigger and stay ahead. Thanks to the copycats, the competitive fire inside me was blazing.

In copycat situations, I always found it best to give myself a few days to vent, cool down, and then revisit the situation with a calmer frame of mind. That meant I had more control over how Schmidt's was perceived—maintaining its reputation as a positive, forward-looking brand—not to mention the fact that I wouldn't have felt right putting anybody down. Instead, I let these incidents provide incentive to work harder. My business thrived best when I focused on it, without getting distracted by copycats.

When you've hit on something exciting, copycats (and haters) are going to show up. Often, the best thing to do is shake it off and keep your eye on your own brand (except in cases of blatant trademark infringements or scenarios that need legal attention).

Patent and trademark when you can

As I became aware of close competitors and unabashed imitators—which happened more and more as the presence of Schmidt's grew—I wanted to protect my creation without losing my sanity. What if I were to patent my recipes?

While my formula wasn't public, my ingredients were. Anyone could pick up a jar of deodorant and see exactly what was in it. That didn't mean someone could necessarily replicate my deodorant, as the specific ratio of ingredients (not to mention the complicated process of heating, mixing, holding, and cooling in a precise way) was proprietary. But what if just knowing my ingredients allowed a competitor to come close to ripping off my recipe?

Part of learning the landscape was learning about the laws surrounding patents and trademarks. Initially, I considered patenting my formula in order to protect it. What I soon learned, though, was that a patent might not help me much, because if someone were to differentiate their formula from mine in even the subtlest of ways—say, using the exact same ingredients but in different ratios—my legal case in protecting my patent would be significantly diminished.

Next, the idea of trademarking came up when I started to spot competitors "borrowing" language from my messaging. A little research helped me figure out that I could trademark my brand name, logo, taglines, phrases, and design elements. Once you trademark something and use it in the marketplace, competitors can't legally use it. That doesn't mean you have to start suing any brand that looks and sounds like yours. Instead, you can send a formal email or letter stating you suspect their messaging, branding, or whatever may be infringing on your trademark. Often that settles the issue quickly.

The full process of filing for a trademark can take up to a year, so we added our "TM" signs early to ward off opportunists or copycats. Trademark law generally protects those who can demonstrate they were the first to use a mark in commerce, and once the filing process is complete, that of course makes it easier to defend.

Later, not long after I trademarked Schmidt's assets, I had to deal with one of the most egregious copycats. By then I'd taken on a few distributors based in the EU. Distributors work with retailers and manufacturers to help your products get to market. It's often easier for retailers to order multiple products directly from a distributor, who serves as a single point of contact, instead of working with multiple brands individually. One of my distributors in the EU was evidently so inspired by Schmidt's that he decided to focus his attention not on landing accounts for us but on creating his own version. The deodorant brand he invented completely ripped off Schmidt's scents, colors, and packaging. There was even a page on the website telling an "about" story of an idealistic young couple—the woman was pregnant—determined to change the way people think about deodorant. It was hard to believe what I was seeing. Customers from the EU emailed, asking, "Is this Schmidt's?" One of the attorneys representing Schmidt's (by then we had several) successfully ordered an injunction, forcing the brand to take their products off shelves. Most of the time trademark infringements are innocent mistakes—but not always. Over the years, having Schmidt's assets trademarked paid off.

Privacy and protection
WAYS TO PROTECT YOUR BRAND

Trademark. Consider trademarking your name and logo, design assets, key messages, and so on.

Be smart with proprietary information. Protect information that's central to your business, like a recipe, by only sharing it with employees who need to know. For example, a person in charge of capping the jars of

Schmidt's deodorant didn't need to know every component of the formula to do her job.

Use nondisclosure agreements. As your business grows, ask contractors, partners, and employees to sign nondisclosure agreements (NDAs) to help ensure proprietary information will not be shared.

Don't make unsubstantiated claims. Competitors might try to knock you out of the running by challenging some of your messaging and/or benefit claims. Keep competitors off your back by monitoring your messaging and only saying what's both 100 percent accurate and legally permissible.

Have a strong contract with your co-packers or contract manufacturers. If your product will be made offsite by a third party, protect your formula with a solid contract. (This is standard practice, of course, but not all contracts are created equally.) You don't have to figure everything out alone; work with an attorney or mentor to help cover your bases.

Claim carefully

When Schmidt's was a relatively small and local brand, big companies hardly paid attention to what I was doing. But as my business grew—especially with its expansion into national retail chains in later years—more customers switched from conventional brands to Schmidt's, and those big brands started taking note.

One day, a piece of certified mail showed up on my doorstep. I opened it to find a legal notice from a big-name brand formally challenging some of our statements about

Schmidt's products. Up to this point, I hadn't realized certain requirements attached to some of the language I was using. For instance, one of our social media posts mentioned that Schmidt's could outlast the competition, which plenty of customers said had been their experience—but I learned this kind of language actually had to be proven in a formal study. Even quoting customers online or in marketing materials, like "Best deodorant ever! —Allie from Texas," could be problematic, because it's viewed as the equivalent of the brand making a claim.

To be clear, I never had any question about the truth and accuracy of these statements. After quickly consulting with an attorney, I understood that some descriptions could be used only if they were supported by surveys or studies. We immediately made some changes in order to avoid any problems.

Today, when I look at new brands and small businesses, I can quickly spot claims that are likely unsupported: statements like "lasts forever," "better and safer than regular deodorants," or even "the best deodorant ever!" I'm sure 99 percent of the time entrepreneurs aren't aware they're breaking any rules; I sure wasn't aware in my early days. But even if it's unintentional and even if you are confident that your statements are accurate or your opinions are actually supported by consumers, as I was, you could still get into trouble. So always do your research, err on the side of caution, and consult a lawyer or attorney who specializes in product claims.

Keep values at the forefront

The longer I ran Schmidt's, the more I accepted that the competition would always be there, and that the best way to deal with it was to stay ahead of them. To do that, I continually trained my focus on the quality of my own product and the strength of my relationships with customers and retailers, as well as my brand and mission. As the business grew, these are some of the strategies Schmidt's employed that I believe helped us keep our edge.

It often served me much better to understand my and my customer's values than to know the ins and outs of my competitors. Once, after shipping an opening order of deodorant to a new shop in Portland, I was dismayed to find multiple stories online about the owners' anti-gay views. I recognized I had an opportunity and obligation to stand by my values as a business owner, and by those of my customers. I notified the shop owner that I was withdrawing as a vendor. Then I went to the store and pulled my products. Yes, I walked into the store and took my products from the shelves. Awkward.

When Schmidt's quickly developed a large following of vegan customers, it was important to me to be mindful of this group's beliefs and high standards. I made it a priority to go through the process of obtaining vegan certification for the products. Additionally, being cruelty free was important to me and my customers, and I was motivated to get Schmidt's certified as cruelty free by the Leaping Bunny program (certification means we don't test on animals and neither do any of our ingredient suppliers). It was a long, arduous process, but it made me proud to have the certification.

Later, when Schmidt's had the opportunity to expand to China—a huge market—I refused, despite being challenged for being "picky" and told sales should come first. I knew the country required mandatory animal testing, and protecting my and my customers' values sometimes meant a possible lost opportunity for the business. Even if there was some way around the testing, it was not something I was willing to budge on, as I wasn't willing to risk the potential misinterpretation by my customers.

Another way Schmidt's stayed ahead was by distinguishing itself with lifestyle branding as our marketing budget grew—that is, by being an early brand to use authentic photography and storytelling that featured real, diverse people captured candidly. It was a departure from the industry norm of showing a sexy model on a spin bike or hitting a punching bag followed by a litany of claims like "Eliminates odor on contact!" or "Lasts for 24 hours without white marks!" Schmidt's was more than a product; it was about the people who believed in a future where natural products were the norm. So instead of focusing on just the qualities of our deodorant, our messaging was more aspirational, rallying customers around a movement to bring natural products to the mainstream. Other deodorant companies were out there to make a buck—we were out there to change the world!

When Schmidt's expanded into more retail locations later in the business, I learned just how valuable my relationship with each store's buyer was. Investing in those relationships meant that some buyers became more like collaborators, and I could even ask things like, "What ingredients are trending?" "In which regions do you see our performance stalling?" "Which of my competitors should I be worried about?" Amazing insights came out of these conversations that helped keep us ahead. Over time, I started to consider these buyers trusted partners, and they saw me that way as well. I also frequently sent press clippings to my retail partners—or businesses I hoped would become retail partners—not just to demonstrate Schmidt's success, but to show I was invested in the relationship and in it for the long haul. Tending to these partnerships, no doubt, aided Schmidt's in establishing strong footholds on retail shelves.

I also used public industry reports, reports generated from retailer and marketing partners, and, soon, paid-for market analysis reports to get a more granular look at customer preferences, competitors' performance, industry trends, and more. Data like this helped inform digital marketing strategies, our approach to retailers, product messaging, and opportunities for reaching specific audiences. We also ran our own surveys on Google all the time to decide on new scents, ingredients to include, which claims were most important to customers, how they liked new packaging, and so forth. When the business was more mature and we had the budget, we worked with a partner company to run more formal studies to (1) determine consumer interests, and (2) test and report on the efficacy of our products, which became critical to supporting important marketing claims we wanted to be able to make to set Schmidt's apart from the rest. Consumer studies are very expensive, so embarking on this journey wasn't possible until later, when the business had grown and we had the budget. The detailed results of these studies allowed us to make and support better marketing claims than ever, so the investment—not to mention the rich data on how Schmidt's performed—was well worth it.

Ultimately, one of the primary reasons that Schmidt's was successful was my commitment to invest in and promote what differentiated it—without getting distracted by competitors' endeavors. ■

What to make of it

 Don't distort your own vision by obsessing over others.

What's most important is making the best possible version of your own product. Keep tabs on the competition, but prevent yourself from losing your way—focus on and prioritize your own work first. It's about innovating, not emulating. At the end of the day, if you want to get ahead, you need to have confidence in what makes your brand and products exceptional.

 Let copycats fuel you.

If you've got copycats in your midst, it probably means you're on to something. It can also stimulate you into evolving and preventing your messaging from becoming stale. There were a few occasions in my experience when using legal power was necessary, but often, what served me best was tuning imitators out. As entrepreneurs, our time is precious and losing sleep or focus over copycats is a cost we need to avoid.

 Channel your protective instincts.

I'm naturally competitive, and when it came to Schmidt's, I embraced that side of myself. It wasn't about knocking anybody else down—I believe that there's room for everybody doing things their own unique way. It was about dedicating myself completely to my business while remaining protective of what I was building.

CHAPTER 6

Embrace expansion.

Be ambitious about the future while managing in-the-moment demands.

A t the outset of 2013, with the product perfected, popularity established, and fresh branding in place, I set my sights on expansion. What followed was a year of many firsts: my first big-name retail accounts, international orders, national press mentions, office space, and more.

As any entrepreneur will tell you, growing a business is at once thrilling and terrifying. Each new "first" corresponds to a challenge or opportunity. My "say yes now, then figure out how" attitude continued to help me as I took on bigger and bigger "firsts," and the practice allowed me to stay focused on what was right in front of me, instead of getting swept up in worries about the future. I never created a one-year, five-year, or ten-year plan. Even though I consider myself a type-A person—trust me, I love lists, organization, and order—I never thought of a formal business plan as a "must" for getting Schmidt's off the ground. For one thing, it seemed nearly impossible to formulate a plan, given the unpredictable pace of growth. But I also found that short-term thinking served me better. Of course, I had a vision of where I wanted to go—to continue to get more deodorant into more people's hands—but if I got too caught up in long-term planning, it caused the immediate strategy to slow down. Instead I responded quickly to opportunities and kept saying yes. I reassured myself that it was okay not to look *too* far ahead, as long as I kept my nose to the grindstone.

Today, when asked about starting and growing my business, that topic of a business plan often comes up. I'm honest about my own light-handed approach. In the maker and entrepreneurial community, I certainly haven't discovered any hard-and-fast rules that *must* be applied when running a small business; everyone needs something different. From my experience, what matters most is rising to the occasion that's right in front of you and taking one step at a time, even if the steps start to feel more like leaps.

Trade up with trade shows

By 2013, I recognized that trade shows were the most efficient way to capture retailers' attention. They offered a perfect opportunity to meet dozens of potential partners over the course of one Saturday or a weekend. Some shows were too expensive for me to attend in those early years, but a few were local and affordable, and I knew I needed to devote more time to them (versus farmers markets) if I wanted to grow. The longer I ran my business, the easier it became to determine the "next level" or next step to take. The more I put myself out there along the way, from talking to retailers to attending shows, the better I knew the landscape of the industry and how to navigate it.

At these multiday events, there were some days when I'd watch buyers and customers breeze toward my booth, then skip me and head straight for a neighboring exhibitor with artisanal soaps or letterpress greeting cards. I once watched a buyer chat up the person next to me (the owner of a lotion brand), then walk away. Feeling desperate, I chased her down, introduced myself, and put a jar of deodorant in her hands. She respectfully declined but commended me for my straightforward approach. Another day, I met a soap vendor who told me his sister was friends with Alicia Silverstone (noted vegan, animal rights activist, and fan of natural products) and he offered to pass along some of my deodorant. Sure, why not? I handed him a jar. I doubted anything would come of it, but I was determined to capitalize on these costly endeavors any way I could, especially when it meant time away from Chris and Oliver.

To maximize Schmidt's exposure at a popular local event called the Better Living Show, I planned to debut two new scents. My baseline formula was down pat, so creating new scents was not a heavy lift, and I loved the creative process. In addition to my existing Ylang-Ylang + Calendula and Cedarwood + Juniper offerings (along with Fragrance Free), customers had been asking for a brighter, fresher scent. I wanted to add something citrusy that would still be unexpected—more unusual and exotic. I loved the vibrance of lime and landed on bergamot as a perfect match. A green citrus fruit with floral undertones, bergamot is known for its use in high-end perfumes. It's uplifting and fresh, but not overpowering. I knew the name itself would look and sound much more interesting than something familiar, like orange or grapefruit.

I started making test batches of deodorant with the new scent at home. After multiple rounds of testing, I perfected the ratio, and Bergamot + Lime became the fourth scent to join the Schmidt's family.

The fifth scent, Lavender + Sage, required a similar process. Even though I'd avoided creating a lavender deodorant because I felt it was overdone in the naturals scene, I had to acknowledge that the scent had a huge appeal among customers. They'd been asking for it, and nearly all of my competitors in the deodorant space offered it, so if I wanted to win people over, I knew I'd need to meet some of them in their comfort zone. Of course, I wanted to put my own spin on things. My customers had come to expect unusual scent combinations from me, and I loved to develop them; it was part of the Schmidt's DNA at this point. In the end, clary sage emerged as the pairing winner. The combination offered the familiar tranquility of lavender with an original, earthy, soothing boost from the sage.

At the Better Living Show (and all local shows), I put a sign at my booth listing the nearby stores that carried Schmidt's, which helped legitimize the brand and give customers confidence that if they bought and fell in love with the product, they could find it again. I also had a big Schmidt's banner and professional signage printed, which elevated the look of my booth. It was a strong conversation starter to be able to tell anyone who stopped by that I was offering two brand new scents that they could try first! (It never hurts to make your customers feel special.) Sometimes I offered a discount to someone who placed a large order, or I gave away an extra sample to someone who was extra enthusiastic, hoping they'd pass it along to a friend. I believed in my product and in the power of people to spread the word about Schmidt's.

In the weeks before the show, I'd also finally figured out a solution to a common customer complaint that scooping the product out of the jar caused some of it to end up under their fingernails. After some pretty extensive research, I discovered miniature plastic spatulas that I could manually place on top of the cooled deodorant before capping. Now people could scoop out the deodorant with the little tool instead of their hands.

The Better Living Show was enormous and much more heavily trafficked than your typical farmers market or craft fair. People loved the new scents, which ended up becoming my top two sellers.

Early tricks of the trade show
MAXIMIZE YOUR TIME ON THE FLOOR

Introduce yourself to event organizers. They can offer tips on how to get the best booth position (and might offer an upgrade), invite you to speak on panels, tell you about sponsorships, and consider you for awards.

Talk to everyone, all day. Beyond retailers and customers, you can meet ingredient suppliers, manufacturers, media, vendors, researchers, product developers, and brokers.

Don't let opportunities pass. Chasing down buyers and putting jars of deodorant into as many hands as possible was a frequent practice of mine, including paying attention to the company listed on name tags of people who walked by.

Let people know you're going to be there *beforehand*. Tease big announcements (like new products or scents), offer incentives to place orders, and set up meetings proactively.

When multiple customers at the Better Living Show mentioned that they wished their local supermarket—New Seasons Market, a popular chain in the Pacific Northwest—carried Schmidt's, I made note of it. I'd approached the New Seasons Market about six months prior but had been turned away. "Let me know when you are in distribution," the buyer had said. In other words, the store didn't want to buy directly from makers like me. They only wanted to buy from those who worked through a distributor. Stores prefer working with distributors because often they get better pricing and can streamline their business by dealing with fewer vendors. I began to see the importance of establishing these relationships and added "find the best distributors" to my growing list of priorities.

After the show, I pulled up the email thread from months before and wrote to New Seasons Market again.

"I just returned from day one of exhibiting at Portland's Better Living Show. I counted nineteen customers who inquired about finding Schmidt's Deodorant at New Seasons Market," I wrote. (I really had tallied nineteen throughout the show. I wasn't lying when I said I liked lists.)

I told the buyer about my new scents and included a link to a blog that had recently featured Schmidt's. The blog post had already generated positive comments from readers, like, "This deodorant is the best I have ever tried and now my son is hooked on it, too!" and "I found Schmidt's at my local farmers market last summer and that is all I have been using since." I pointed those out, as well.

To conclude my request, I wrote that I'd personally commit to staying on top of inventory and stocking stores, and offered free delivery, no distributor necessary. I also offered to provide references from other retailers.

It was enough to catch the buyer's attention, and she told me she'd put Schmidt's on her to-do list. But when I didn't hear back from her, I again followed up, this time after attending another festival. "At least half of the shoppers I've been talking to are asking whether they can find our product at New Seasons Market," I wrote. "The conversation generally goes like this:

Shopper: "Where can I buy this locally when I run out?"

Me: "Where do you shop?"

Shopper: "New Seasons."

Me: "You can find us at all the food co-ops and many other retailers. We're still working on New Seasons!"

It worked! Even though I didn't yet have a distributor, the buyer made an exception for me. About a year after my sending that follow-up email, Schmidt's found a home on New Seasons' shelves. Later, New Seasons became the first retailer to carry travel-size versions of my deodorant. The store placed bins of the colorful jars near checkout counters, and they quickly became impulse buys for people tempted to give natural a try—a perfect opportunity for exposure.

When we received notice from our landlord about a substantial increase in rent, Chris and I began searching for another rental nearby. We found a little one-story house just around the corner that included a mother-in-law suite in the back. We knew just what I'd use the tiny studio for: Schmidt's headquarters. I was so excited to expand from the kitchen nook I'd been using to pour, label, and pack. When we moved, I set up the studio with a hot plate and a big pot for mixing, and card tables for staging the jars and pouring the deodorant. The cupboards filled up with blocks of cocoa and shea butter and bags of baking soda. I had my own little production space!

Get help brokering deals

As I pitched more and more retailers, I was so anxious to hear back that sometimes I'd sit in front of my laptop just waiting for email responses to come in. Chris set up a voice-activated system so that while I was stirring up deodorant in the kitchen, my laptop would read incoming emails aloud to me. "We are interested in carrying your deodorant," a robotic voice would chime, and I'd do a little jig in my pajamas.

When I'd take important calls with potential accounts at home, I'd pray little Oliver would keep quiet during the conversation. I'd run around our tiny house, trying to put distance between the phone and his giggles or gleeful screams. Oliver thought it was a fun game of "Chase Mommy" and would follow me from room to room, laughing wildly.

Schmidt's filled my schedule completely, and it was getting more and more difficult to juggle it all: the hours at trade shows and market and fair booths, corresponding with buyers over email, making deodorant, packing and shipping deodorant, sending newsletters, and checking in on social media.

Then, in early summer, Mia, a local broker who'd discovered Schmidt's at a farmers market, reached out to see if I wanted sales help. Brokers liaise with retailers on behalf of a brand to help get the product on shelves, making a commission on any deals they successfully land. They're like outsourced salespeople for your company. I started with smaller, independent brokers like Mia to manage specific regions.

Then, once my brand's reputation was solid enough, I was qualified to catch the attention of a large, reputable firm who handled accounts across the country. When Mia contacted me, it was honestly the first time I'd thought about someone helping me with that kind of thing; she spoke a language I didn't yet, and I could learn from her. I brought her on—we agreed to a commission we both felt was fair—and we began meeting weekly at a coffee shop in the neighborhood.

Mia had worked in the beauty and personal care industry for a while and had connections to retailers she thought would be a good fit for Schmidt's, including national chain grocery stores like Sprouts. With the elevated look I'd achieved with the rebrand, she also saw potential to position Schmidt's as a luxury beauty item that could be carried in boutiques and lifestyle stores like Anthropologie, Urban Outfitters, and other non-grocery retailers, as well as in subscription beauty boxes. Mia generously shared sample line sheets with me so that I could fine-tune mine to better attract attention. Chris spiffed those up for us and added more information for retailers, like my brand story, testimonials, product descriptions, and high-quality photos, so the paperwork had a more elevated and personal feel instead of simply focusing on pricing. Armed with updated materials, Mia was off to the races, nailing new accounts left and right.

Embrace the buzz— and generate your own

One day, the *Portland Tribune* called. By now Schmidt's was well known in town, and the paper must have caught wind of the business and decided to cover my story. A reporter interviewed me at home and snapped a few pictures as I poured a fresh batch of deodorant into jars at my kitchen table. When the article came out, the moment was surreal: there I was in print. The reporter had even called the Alberta Street Co-op to get a quote from one of my contacts there, who said, "People come in, asking for it by name . . . We love Schmidt's Deodorant so much that it's a permanent Staff Pick. Many of us are devoted customers of Jaime's." I gushed with pride, and when the paper hit newsstands I bought ten copies, mailing one to my parents. Growing up, if ever I was in the local newspaper for getting on the honor roll or doing well in a tennis match, my dad always carefully cut out the article, laminated it, and added it to a folder he kept—he had one for me and one for my brother, Jason. I knew he'd be proud to see the *Tribune* feature. (Both he and my brother had only ever used conventional deodorant in the past, and neither had any amount of interest in natural products. They weren't exactly my target audience, so when both had tried Schmidt's and liked it enough to "convert," I knew I was on to something.)

Around the same time, the popular TV show *Portlandia* created a skit called "Mother's Sun Deodorant" that poked fun at natural deodorant. Not only was it really funny, but it was an obvious parody of Schmidt's (they mentioned Schmidt's on their blog when the episode aired). The fact that my company had become big enough to be part of the broader cultural conversation (even in a joking way) felt like proof I was making a dent.

These early press moments came about organically, but soon Mia kicked off what would later become an important strategy for Schmidt's: blogger and influencer outreach. Her marketing efforts were another service she offered in addition to brokering. We wanted to see if we could start getting a little more press attention to attract new customers and build awareness, but we knew we weren't quite at a stage where large outlets and magazines would feature us. It's tough to land big placements like that unless you know an editor or they reach out to you first. So instead, Mia began pitching beauty blogs and influencers, hoping to generate buzz. At the same time, she connected with contributing and freelance writers on LinkedIn—ones who often wrote about personal care or beauty trends—so if the occasion arose, she could pitch Schmidt's. Instead of sending a cold email to a hotshot editor at a big outlet, we hoped approaching writers would be a better strategy to get us in the door. In time, the strategy led to blog features, increased web sales, and growth in our social presence.

Outreach strategy
WAYS TO GENERATE BUZZ WITHOUT A PR AGENCY

Samples, samples, samples. Send them to writers, bloggers, and influencers of all levels, and prepare to follow up. In our packages, we also included a lookbook with lifestyle and product photos, the brand story with my photo, press mentions, and the products. People frequently commented on how much they loved it.

Contact writers on social media. Emails can get lost or overlooked, so what sometimes works better is simply commenting on posts or DMing.

Make friends. Create connections with other brands and founders, especially at events. Once I was chatting with a fellow founder at a trade show when a journalist he knew walked up and joined us. We were introduced, and shortly after, that journalist wrote a feature about me.

Think big. Establish partnerships and purpose-driven campaigns with other organizations. Collaborations like these benefit customers, widen your network, and can attract media attention.

Share unbranded content. Talking only about your product can get old. Blog about industry trends (for us, that meant other natural personal care trends and topics), which shows customers (and the press) that you have a deep understanding of and investment in the industry. Later, Schmidt's launched *The Natural*, a lifestyle editorial site exploring all things wellness.

With Mia proactively corresponding with retailers and handling outreach efforts, I was freed up to focus on production and shipping, which were becoming increasingly time consuming. Even with my bigger pot, I could only make about twenty jars of deodorant in a given batch (and up to about 150 jars in a typical workday), and with each new retail account, that meant more time in the studio. Then, in June, totally out of the blue, I received a phone call from a retailer in the Netherlands. (Yes, I had my personal number listed on the website.) I hardly ever answered the phone—instead letting voicemail do its job—in large part because of my unstable voice. But I was intrigued by this call coming from another country, so I picked up. The person on the line said she'd learned about Schmidt's on Pinterest, where someone had compared it to another natural deodorant brand she carried in her shop. Based on that one pin, which claimed Schmidt's was better than the other brand, she wanted to place an order for five hundred jars. I nearly dropped the phone. At the time, I was producing much less than that in an entire month. How would I make and ship it all? I wasn't sure, but you can probably guess what I did: "Yes!" I said, then figured out how.

She told me I could invoice her up front (which is not always the case), and I agreed to cover the cost of shipping since that was my existing policy for an order of that size. (After that hefty expense, I realized I'd need a different policy for international orders.) I told her it would take me a week to make the deodorant, and I got to work. After a series of long days, I made my way through the slog of producing five hundred jars of deodorant—in addition to what I had to produce for my existing accounts—and capped and boxed up all of them, reusing the boxes the empty jars came in (which came with snug inserts that kept the glass jars from knocking against one another—I was always looking for ways to keep costs down through reuse).

But what about the temperature during the journey? I was worried about my deodorants melting, especially in summer. Once the formula melted, it could easily leak, and when it cooled again, the texture was never quite the same. The small shipments I made for Etsy or website orders had made it to customers in good shape, but this was no ordinary shipment. I went to the store and checked out dry ice, but when I burnt my finger in the process, I got intimidated and decided not to use it. It would have to be a leap of faith. Chris's mom came over and helped me load up the car with three big, heavy boxes. The two of us, plus Oli, drove to FedEx, and I strode in and proudly announced that I had a big international order to ship. The woman at the counter looked at me, unfazed, and handed over a form to fill out. When my little deodorants were finally accepted and on their way across the globe, Oliver, Chris's mom, and I went to a nearby Mexican restaurant and celebrated with margaritas (Oliver had apple juice). I tracked that order every day until it arrived, thankfully, in perfect condition.

Bring in help

I loved being the one and only creator of my product, so I put off giving up control. But after getting through the Netherlands shipment, and with new retail accounts steadily coming in, it was becoming clear I couldn't continue to keep up with demand by myself. Working so closely with Mia showed me the real benefits of collaboration, too.

The first time I had hired help was the friend I brought on a for a few weeks (the one with the copycat girlfriend). After that, I began looking for longer-term employees: someone to help with packing and shipping, and another to help with producing deodorant. I asked around and found Ben through a recommendation from Mia. After a quick email exchange, I told Ben he was hired. (There was no time to mess around! And he turned out to be one of Schmidt's longest-term employees.) His role—which would be packing deodorant for shipment from my garage—started as one shift a week and quickly grew to three full days, and within just a few weeks, became a full-time job.

Ben quickly proved to be a steadfast, reliable, and independent worker. The garage was somewhat dark and dank, but he put on sports radio and didn't seem to mind. He'd pack each box, small or large, in an orderly fashion, then help load them into my car at the end of the day in the alley behind our house. I was now trekking daily to the post office with a carload of deodorant. Upon arrival, I'd be greeted with flat smiles from postal workers who surely dreaded my and Oliver's massive and increasingly regular delivery right before closing.

Next I brought on Alex, a good friend of Chris's, to handle production. I showed him my little studio in the back and walked him through the process of measuring, melting, pouring, and labeling. He picked it up right away, and together we formed a loose system in which I'd tell him how much deodorant I needed by when, and he'd come by to make it as it suited his schedule. He was happiest when left alone to work with his punk and hardcore playlists blasting at full volume (but was always open to sharing lunch in the kitchen with Chris and me if we were cooking something up that day), and his unconventional shifts didn't bother me; Alex quickly impressed me by churning out consistent batches on time. He was a hard worker, trustworthy, and reliable.

With Ben and Alex on board, I forgot about the initial anxiety I'd felt about losing control. It was a huge relief.

Hiring for fit
WHAT TO BE MINDFUL OF AS YOU BUILD YOUR TEAM

Referrals. For the first employee or two, you may find comfort in hiring acquaintances or referrals. But, as the company grows, it is important to have other considerations, like those that follow.

Passion. Pay attention to candidates who demonstrate a real passion and excitement for your brand. Not every hire will have previous experience that aligns precisely with the job (there were no former deodorant mixers for me to hire). But ones who brought enthusiasm and creative ideas to the application and interview process often got in the door. Many of my most successful hires were those I chose for their demonstrated commitment and excitement around the brand.

Initiative. Look for someone willing to jump in and put new systems into place at a startup or smaller company, rather than someone looking for a more stable workplace with clear procedures and expectations. Some people came into an interview ready to list their accomplishments and achievements, but it was more impactful when they could instead show they understood how their skills could positively impact Schmidt's.

Growth mindset. Hire people who are interested in growing and developing along with the company. The most rewarding thing for me as a boss was to see employees evolve and take charge of their personal career path within the company, and I always loved to support them however I could.

Synchronicity. Hires who innately understood the mission of the company and whose values and goals harmonized with my own were generally most successful.

Spend it to make it

With Ben and Alex's help, I also had much more time to communicate with retailers and buyers, as well as with customers.

As I continued expanding to new retail accounts and gaining more customers—who'd never met me at a booth, and who were new to natural deodorant—more questions and comments appeared on social media and Etsy at all hours. "What does Bergamot + Lime smell like?" "How do you put it on?" "Are these available near me?" Questions like these, though valid and easy to answer, started requiring more and more of my time. Almost without realizing it, I'd become Schmidt's one-woman customer support team.

It was important to have my eye on these accounts as much as possible, not just to respond to customers, but also to keep track of potential opportunities. One day I noticed the owner of a company called Vegan Cuts commenting on an Instagram post saying she loved my deodorant. After corresponding with her through comments, I got her contact information and emailed her. Vegan Cuts had an ecommerce site and box subscription program featuring vegan products. The owner offered to include Schmidt's in one of its beauty boxes, which had about a thousand subscribers. In tandem with the box offering, Vegan Cuts would also put Schmidt's up for sale on its site and promote us to its one hundred thousand total subscribers. It seemed like an amazing opportunity.

But even though Schmidt's was growing by leaps and bounds, I still wasn't closely tracking finances. I knew the money coming in from retail accounts and markets was more than enough to cover supplies, plus Ben's and Alex's hourly rates, but I wasn't paying myself any specific amount, and I still hadn't begun to think about a formal budget for marketing, advertising, or unique opportunities such as this one. In an email to Mia, I proposed sending Vegan Cuts a thousand jars of deodorant (at no cost), as they'd suggested.

She was quick to discourage me, instead suggesting we offer "minis"—small, travel-sized versions. Mia wrote:

> *I'm going to assume that your COGS [cost of goods sold] are around two dollars to make a full-size deodorant. One thousand free full-size pieces would cost you $2,000 to GIVE AWAY. And also, in giving a full-size product away to one thousand subscribers, you essentially cancel the demand for one thousand potential sales . . . The minis still allow one thousand subscribers to try the product and STILL remain inclined to make a full-size purchase.*

She was right. I calculated how long I thought it would take to make enough deodorant and fill a thousand mini jars, plus the cost of shipping, and felt comfortable green lighting the opportunity. I was thrilled at how the team worked together strategically on it. There was no saying for sure what kind of sales would result, but the exposure—specifically among this target audience of vegan customers—seemed worth the investment. From the get-go, Schmidt's had attracted a customer base of vegans who loved my safe, cruelty-free formula. In general, vegans were a particularly engaged, connected group, and approval among this audience spread rapidly by word of mouth, especially from YouTube influencers.

After the boxes went out, Vegan Cuts surveyed recipients to ask how they liked Schmidt's. The responses were overwhelmingly positive: most said they "loved it," 45 percent said they planned to buy it (and a few dozen already had through Vegan Cuts' site), and 70 percent said they'd refer Schmidt's to a friend. Some wished to see it in stick form, a comment I often heard and knew one day I would address. We ended up working with Vegan Cuts again for several additional campaigns. With each one, I received a similar report with survey results so I could track performance and hear from different customer segments. Later, I partnered with Birchbox and other subscription boxes, too, which were instrumental in spreading the word about Schmidt's. For a consumable brand like mine, I found the investment to be well worth it.

Not long after Mia came on board, I connected with Lisa, a Seattle-based broker who said she had a contact at Whole Foods. That got my attention (Whole Foods!) and I brought her on. Often brokers work by region, and in this case, Mia could handle the Portland area while Lisa covered Seattle.

Various representatives from Whole Foods had stopped by my booth at markets over the years, and I was eager to land that account. (As discussed earlier, trade shows are a great place to meet reps.) Between my efforts and Lisa's, I was finally getting close. That summer, a Whole Foods analyst who'd picked up a jar of deodorant at one of my weekend booths emailed me: "I have got to say . . . of all of the natural deodorants I have tried in my life . . . and there have been many, yours is by far head and shoulders above the rest!" If there was ever a pat-yourself-on-the-back moment, this was one. She promised to bring up Schmidt's when she talked with the regional buyer in their next meeting. Lisa completed the required forms and spreadsheets, providing details about the product's weight, dimensions, barcodes, price, and much more. With everything submitted, I crossed my fingers (and toes, and everything else) and waited. When the news arrived that I was officially accepted for placement in Whole Foods' Pacific Northwest region, I was elated. Each retail account was a milestone, but Whole Foods was truly a behemoth landmark.

As I prepared to work with Whole Foods, I learned their free-fill policy applied to units under ten dollars—which included my deodorant jars—and meant Schmidt's wouldn't see a penny from the whole opening order. A case of each scent went to fourteen stores, or 420 total units. I tried to negotiate, but when I didn't get anywhere, I had to accept that this was how things worked, and I proceeded anyway. I was optimistic Schmidt's would sell well, and there was no way I was going to turn down an opportunity at Whole Foods. I knew we'd soon be making money from the account—and sure enough, we did, with Schmidt's actually becoming their top-selling deodorant!

Make space to grow

In October, I received an email that made me do a double take. It was *Us Weekly* contacting me to say that they were working on a story about celebrities' favorite products, and that Alicia Silverstone had mentioned Schmidt's. The jar I'd handed the soap vendor at the show months earlier had actually made its way to her? I was stunned. The shout-out became a pivotal moment for the business. On the day the issue hit mailboxes across the country, I remember driving to my mother-in-law's house to pick up Oliver, and my phone began pinging over and over and over. Each notification was an email alerting me to a new website order. I drove the whole way with an enormous smile on my face. I had received my first major celebrity endorsement and it was in print for all to see. Looking out at the starry sky, I realized big things were on the horizon—I could feel it.

The week of the feature, I sold over five hundred units online. Up to that point, I'd been processing about a few hundred orders per *month* through the website. The volume was completely overwhelming, and I was tempted to put up a "sold out" notice, but couldn't face the possibility of missing out on any new customers. So Alex, Ben, and I powered through—the beginning of a common theme at our office.

It was obvious it was no longer tenable to produce and package all this deodorant from my home. A commercial space around the corner had put up a "for lease" sign, and I called the building owner. With a shaky voice, I described my business to him, a little nervous that he might not take me seriously. I was having a monumental year, and even though I was eager and determined to build on my success, frankly, I wasn't fully confident I could afford a lease.

Still, my intuition—not to mention the claustrophobic state of my studio—told me it was time to commit myself to expansion, and I signed the lease on the very first Schmidt's production space/office/warehouse in the fall of 2013. It was a small 750-square-foot space, but it was a huge improvement, and the rent turned out to be only a few hundred dollars a month. The landlord helped me set up the interior and let me paint a wall Schmidt's red (even helping, in exchange for a bottle of whisky). I scheduled USPS and UPS pickups, so Ben and I wouldn't need to load up my car and make trips to the post office—which was a *huge* improvement to our process. With more space, it was also much easier to store supplies, and buying in bulk helped me save money. I could order larger quantities of jars online, as well as bigger orders of cocoa and shea butter, which I was buying from a local supplier. My baking soda at this point still came from Costco and my arrowroot from Bob's Red Mill; we procured many of our essential oils, waxes, and butters from a local supplier as well. Every week, Chris would pick up dozens of the heavy, bulky bags and boxes, receiving weird looks from customers and cashiers. Soon, we started ordering pallet deliveries directly to our new space, saving on time and money.

Bulking up
TIPS FOR WORKING WITH SUPPLIERS (WITHOUT GOING BROKE)

Everything's negotiable. Suppliers may present you with their "standard" price, but it's often negotiable. Payment terms are too. Many will ask that you pay up front for materials, but you can ask for thirty, sixty, or even ninety-day payment terms. This will allow you to use the cash flow to operate rather than having to pay up front for ingredients you haven't yet made into product and turned into income.

Build trust. Sometimes it's easier to negotiate once a relationship is in place, after you've proven that you're a consistent buyer. What can help is to tell the supplier up front that you're working with a specific retailer (like Whole Foods), conveying you anticipate spending a lot of money with them to fulfill orders.

Strategize on inventory. Use reports/analytics to predict how much you should buy. You need to make sure you have enough room to store ingredients and use them fast enough so they stay fresh. Even though bigger orders can get you bigger discounts, don't go too far with too much money tied up in raw materials. A procurement consultant can help you establish a system for replenishing inventory.

Have backups. If you're on a tight schedule and one of your suppliers is out of stock or has an issue, that can create a problem. Have backup suppliers just in case.

One night, as I walked through the front door at home, my phone buzzed. It was an email from Mia with huge news: Schmidt's had been accepted into Anthropologie. I couldn't believe it. It had been a year since I rebranded, and landing Anthropologie felt like real validation the investment had been worth it. Schmidt's not only worked, but it looked beautiful enough to sit on shelves at a place like Anthropologie. As I read the words on my screen, Oliver, who'd heard me come through the door, ran up with a big smile on his face, arms outstretched. "Mommy!" he exclaimed. I dropped down to my knees and pulled him close to my chest, wrapping my arms around him. The timing was perfect; we celebrated the moment together.

Oliver was almost four years old now, in preschool, and forever blowing me away with his sweetness, curiosity, creativity, and charm—more so with each day. Recently I'd found huge crayon marks on a wall in the living room (he loved to draw). When I called Oliver over and asked, "What did you use to draw on the walls?" he looked at me with his big hazel eyes and said, "My imagination." It was all I could do not to burst into laughter. I had to hand it to him—the kid certainly was creative. With my workdays becoming longer and longer, I worried about having enough time and energy for Oliver. Even though my schedule was relatively flexible, being an entrepreneur could be all-consuming (even at the moment I found out we got Anthropologie, I was thinking, *If we can get them, that means we need to go after Urban Outfitters*). What helped was routine. I was strict with myself about sitting down for dinner every night with Chris and Oliver, and maintaining a nightly bedtime ritual with Oliver, without fail. It created stability for all of us (and maybe even soothed me as much as it did Oli).

As 2013 wound to a close, I at last set up a business bank account and digital bookkeeping system (QuickBooks), recognizing that I needed to handle payroll in a more organized, systematic way, especially for taxes. It also allowed me to accept retailer payments by credit card for the first time (though many still sent in paper checks). Up to that point, I'd been that person standing at the ATM depositing a huge stack of paper checks one by one, while a line formed behind me, acknowledging everyone's annoyance with an uncomfortable chuckle and "Almost done!" I had also been buying all raw materials with my personal money and wasn't closely tracking profit. (And yes, this problematic style of record-keeping caused headaches later.) Thanks to my new system, I was able to calculate that I'd sold $132,000 worth of deodorant in 2013. And with new accounts like Anthropologie coming in, I knew I was about to sell far more. I took Ben and Alex out for a drink at O'Malley's, the dive bar around the corner, to celebrate. It was the first Schmidt's company holiday party. ∎

What to make of it

 Own your ambition.

With each milestone I reached, my personal ambition to make Schmidt's as widely available as possible emerged as a driving philosophy for the company. Because I wanted everyone to have access to safe products, we cultivated an expansive list of sales channels—from online to subscription box to mom and pop—when many of our competitors had only one or two.

 Don't look *too* far ahead.

Short-term thinking always served me better than a traditional long-term business plan. Understanding where you're going is key, but if you get too caught up in the long-term plan, it can suppress the immediate strategy. In the beginning, responding quickly to opportunities helped me gain traction.

 Find your balance between entrepreneurship and family life.

As Oliver grew up, so did the business, and it demanded more of me. Creating balance was an ever-evolving effort. I was mindful of the kinds of conversations Chris and I had in front of him; I didn't want Oliver worried about Schmidt's operations or finances. But I often asked if he wanted to weigh in on scents and product ideas, which he loved. All the while, staying consistent in our routines (like dinner and bedtime) steadied us, and Oli became adept at telling me when to put down my phone.

Make an

Impact

Change the landscape
+ disrupt an industry

CHAPTER 7

An open mind opens doors.

Show up fully, and be prepared for the unexpected.

O n January 14, 2014, I boarded a plane to New York City—a place I'd never been—to film a segment for Fox News. I sat by myself in coach, too nervous to read or eat or do much of anything except stare out the window. The thought of being on national television was entirely surreal. A write-up in the local paper or in a blog was one thing, and a magazine shout-out from Alicia Silverstone was another, but this was a whole new ball game.

When Fox first emailed, my initial reaction was *no way.* What if I went on TV and my voice failed? I'd become skilled at managing my vocal condition in my everyday life, and, while problematic, it didn't entirely inhibit me while speaking with customers. (If my voice got warbly, I'd simply say, "Pardon me, I'm getting over a cold.") But exposing my unpredictable voice to the entire world on TV was another story, and nerves made the issue worse. For high-pressure calls with potential retail accounts, I always went for a walk beforehand to help calm me down and keep my voice steady. The method was far from perfect, though, and as soon as I could, I tasked Ben with handling incoming calls while I communicated by my preferred method: email.

I forwarded the Fox email to Mia and asked if she'd do the interview in my place. "Jaime, nobody wants to see *me*!" she said. "They want to see *you*." *I* was Schmidt's. I had committed myself to being the living embodiment—founder, CEO, spokesperson—of the brand, even when that meant facing a very real, very personal challenge that made me feel completely vulnerable. Mia was right: nobody else could take my place.

I couldn't have known it then, but going on Fox News would become a pivotal moment in the life of my business— and one I almost missed.

Prep for press

When I arrived at LaGuardia Airport, I was greeted by a private driver, which I thought was the coolest thing (he even had a "Schmidt" sign). It was after dark when I arrived, and as we drove to my hotel in Times Square, I gaped at the blur of lights, people, and skyscrapers, amazed and overwhelmed by the idea that I was here because of the success of my own business. Fox had contacted me out of the blue (I never did find out how I got on their radar), but I took it as confirmation Schmidt's was making an impact well beyond Portland.

I had to be at the studio the next morning by 9:30 A.M., which already had me feeling uneasy, because it was so early back home on West Coast time. The show I'd be featured on was called *A Healthy You & Carol Alt*. Carol, a supermodel-turned-wellness-guru, would interview me about what made my natural deodorant safer than traditional ones. I'd been told we'd discuss why it's good to avoid certain chemicals in deodorant, along with details about my product and how it adds to a healthy lifestyle. Based on that, I had a few talking points prepared, mostly about "problem" ingredients commonly found in traditional deodorants, and why I avoided them. Beyond that, I wasn't sure what to expect. I planned to wake up early to practice. I'd been instructed to wear "business casual," so I packed black pants and a new blue blouse I bought for the occasion. I also brought a little bag of herbal remedies, including throat lozenges, essential oils, and magnesium, hopeful they would help stabilize my voice. In the morning I'd rehearse, eat a healthy breakfast, take my remedies, and try to remain calm.

When I woke up the next morning and looked at the clock, my heart dropped into my stomach. Somehow my alarm hadn't gone off, or in my jet-lagged state I'd slept right through it. Either way, it was over an hour later than I'd planned to wake up. Frantic, I jumped out of bed, rushed to get ready, and headed for the studio with my little bag in tow, barely making it on time. I had no chance to practice my speaking points over breakfast as I'd hoped.

When I walked through the doors of the studio, it was pretty surreal. I felt like I had no business being there. Thankfully, sitting in hair and makeup gave me a chance to relax before filming. The stylist was chatty and warm, and talking with him as he ironed my hair and powdered my face put me at ease. I'd never had my makeup done professionally and wanted to make sure I still looked like me. "Easy on the foundation," I reminded him more than once. Next I was shown to a waiting area, where a TV played the current studio recording live as it happened. I watched Carol Alt interview the guest before me—a woman who, of course, was perfectly articulate and well spoken.

Then it was time. I thought for sure there'd be a dry run or rehearsal, but to my alarm, there wasn't. A crew member walked me on set and showed me where to stand next to Carol, on a tiny tape "x." Carol shook my hand and introduced herself with a warm smile, exuding poise and confidence. Jars of my deodorant sat on a waist-high podium between us, all five scents. I thought we all might melt under the lights. And just like that, it was time to start rolling.

The producer counted down, the camera zoomed in on Carol, and she began reading her lines from the teleprompter. "Have you ever been on a bus or train or crowded room and thought, *Oh my, does that person stink? Why don't they put on some deodorant?* Well, wearing deodorant or antiperspirant filled with chemicals is not always ideal . . ." As I listened to Carol speak, I made an effort to smile and look natural, but I felt totally dorky and out of my element on stage. Plus, it was hard to focus on Carol when I was trying to keep in mind what I wanted to say. Then I heard my name and realized Carol was introducing me: "Hi, Jaime, welcome! Glad you're here!"

"Thank you for having me," I said, and smiled nervously into the camera.

Carol spoke about the hazards of aluminum, parabens, and phthalates, and invited me to talk about my own ingredients. I'd prepared statements I knew I wanted to make and, although nervous, I felt prepared. After all, I'd been researching and talking about and making deodorant for years. This was *my thing.*

But when the words came out, I didn't sound like the confident, passionate person I was. Instead, my voice kept breaking. Even though I stood tall, smiled broadly, and was as well informed as anybody could be when it came to my ingredients, I couldn't control my shaky, strained voice.

When it was over, I immediately asked the crew if we could do another take. I leaned over to Carol and told her, "I'm not as nervous as I sound, I just have this condition with my voice." She smiled kindly and quickly reassured me; then we started again from the top, going through the same questions. At the end, I still wasn't satisfied and asked for another take. Crew members glanced at one another and looked at the clock. After three or four times, an assistant walked up to me and said, "We have to move on," ushering me back to the waiting room.

I sat down, flooded by a mix of emotions. I was relieved it was over, but terrified that I had done horribly. I'd been told the segment would air in a few weeks, but what if they opted not to air it at all? When the assistant came back out, I pulled her aside and tried to explain my voice condition in full.

"It's okay! You were great!" she said. "You'll get better with time."

I felt like no one understood what I was saying (in more ways than one). I hung around the waiting area for a while, not ready to accept that I couldn't have one more take to get it right. Finally, I left, resigned to wait and see what would happen. I stepped out into the busy streets of NYC and tried to forget about it.

In early February, a few weeks after filming, the segment aired. Chris and I streamed it at home on his desktop computer in the living room while my parents dialed in on speakerphone. My parents were so happy for me that I'd found a purpose in Schmidt's, though at times they were definitely a little confused or concerned by my "deodorant business." "So, are you still selling deodorant?" my mom would ask whenever we spoke on the phone. Later, when Schmidt's became available at retailers near them, they'd go out of their way to stop by stores and straighten up the product on shelves. And when I got my first meeting with Meijer, a big supermarket chain headquartered in Michigan, they drove me three hours each way from their home in Frankenmuth, sitting in the waiting room while I gave my presentation.

When Carol Alt looked into the camera and started talking about deodorant, my heart began to race—this was it. The camera cut to a wider view and there I was, standing across from Carol in my blue blouse. I wasn't used to seeing my hair straightened and smoothed so dramatically. It was beyond strange to see my face on screen.

But when I heard my voice, I broke into tears. I walked out of the room, unable to watch. I was so embarrassed. How could I have thought I'd magically be unaffected by my vocal condition on national TV?

As I began to get swept away in a spiral of negative thoughts, the phone rang. Chris called me over and put my parents on hold so I could answer. I couldn't believe it when the person on the line said they were watching me on TV and wanted to hear more about my deodorant. The segment wasn't even over yet! Immediately afterwards, another customer called, followed by another. Some had questions about the scents or wanted to place an order, but many just wanted to talk deodorant. And the calls kept coming. One person told me she never knew aluminum in deodorant could be harmful; another told me his whole life history of dealing with body odor. However quirky, each caller was curious, appreciative, and kind. I talked as long as they wanted. My voice, while not perfect, was calmer and smoother, and it was comforting to connect with customers on an intimate level, just as I'd done from day one at the farmers market. This was what it had always been about. I started to relax.

While calls streamed through on the phone, orders—several thousand of them—flooded the website. I was beside myself with excitement. *Thousands* of people from all across the country were buying my deodorant. Now I just had to make and ship it, which was clearly not going to be an easy feat. Ben, who rarely traveled, happened to be away that weekend. On top of that, a rare snowstorm had just come through Portland, and the roads were completely undriveable. How was I going to fulfill all these orders? I called Ben in a panic and said, "We're screwed."

Portland is a city without snowplows, and I was the only one who could get to our production space just a few blocks away, so I put on my boots and trudged through the snow. Once there, I started to process orders, using a popular web-based system that was terribly slow and inefficient. At the time, there wasn't a way to batch-process orders, so I had to go through each order manually, one by one, clicking through a series of screens. For every order I processed, four new ones would come through in the meantime. There was no way I could get ahead.

The next day, dependable Alex arrived by bus after a painstakingly long commute on the snowy roads. When we'd moved into our space just a couple of months earlier, I had ordered a forty-five-gallon mixing pot that allowed us to heat the formula to a precise temperature and stir it with an industrial mixer. The only problem was, it wasn't set up yet. Ben, Alex, and I simply hadn't had time, and I naively didn't anticipate the immediate impact the Fox segment would have. As a result, Alex was still making all the deodorant in an eight-gallon pot on a hot plate. We were so swamped and overloaded with orders that he offered to pull an all-nighter to catch up. In his delirious state, he accidentally mixed bergamot with sage and lime with lavender. I donated the unsellable but perfectly usable product to a friend, a local maker of soap, who told me she'd be happy to share it with her friends and family. It was a financial loss, but it was my fault for expecting sleep deprivation not to have an impact.

For weeks, the onslaught of orders kept coming. At one point the website crashed. Customers were wondering why their deodorant was taking so long to ship, sending me "Where is my order?" emails.

Mia's husband, Gabe, came in to help install a program called ShipStation, which allowed us to batch-process orders and notify customers of shipping updates—a huge improvement. My in-laws helped pack orders into boxes, and I hired a temp to help us label. Chris held down everything at home, cooking our meals and caring for Oliver, while I worked long hours alternating between capping jars, applying labels, and dealing with emails. Tons were flooding my inbox, not just from customers, but from brokers, retailers, and random contacts who wanted to partner with the brand in some way—even a NASCAR driver who wanted to talk about a Schmidt's sponsorship.

After a few weeks of sleepless nights and all-hands-on-deck mania, we caught up on orders, set up our new machinery, and regained our sanity. Once we were through the storm, I finally had a chance to reflect on what the Fox News feature had done—and could still do—for my business. Online orders were at a higher volume than ever, and inbound interest from retailers was about to get Schmidt's on many, many more shelves across the country. Going on TV showed me what to expect for future press appearances, and I learned how quickly media attention could snowball: outlets that had seen me on Fox were more likely to take Schmidt's seriously and want to feature us, which created more buzz for the brand. Plus, now I could show customers and retailers the nationwide attention we were getting, which in turn boosted our legitimacy. Once I recovered from the whirlwind, I was completely exhilarated by the potential.

Invest in your online sales strategy

Much of my efforts up to early 2014 had been in establishing relationships with regional and national retailers who could stock my deodorant on store shelves. I'd been selling my product online and was conscientious about maintaining a digital presence and audience on social media, but I had never made it a priority, and hadn't yet invested the time or budget into exploring its full potential. With thousands of people across the country suddenly flocking to the website, it was time to expand my strategy.

In that realm, the first behemoth to address was Amazon. Before the Fox News feature, a woman running an Amazon shop had been placing bulk wholesale orders with me, then reselling my product on the platform. At first, I simply treated her like another retail account. I sold her Schmidt's at my wholesale price and let her do her thing on Amazon. I was simply happy to be available on a channel I didn't have time to manage.

But looking at the invoices, I realized she was one of my biggest buyers. It was clear I was missing out on a huge swath of online customers. And after Fox, other Amazon sellers came out of the woodwork. A huge new audience was going online looking for Schmidt's, and they wanted to capitalize on it. Instead of letting third-party vendors continue to reap profits on my product, it became clear I needed to start selling on Amazon myself.

I needed help, and not just with Amazon, but with my entire direct-to-consumer strategy. Chris had always helped with Schmidt's, from running to Costco to pick up bags of baking soda, to building my first website and then upgrading it, as well as supporting my design and social media endeavors. Early in 2014, he had made a small investment in Facebook and Google ads, just to see what would happen, and they had resulted in tenfold sales. I gave Chris more money for more ads, and the results compounded, making it apparent that digital marketing was a worthwhile endeavor.

Understand your ad/ social platforms

MOST OF SCHMIDT'S AD/SOCIAL SPEND SPANNED ACROSS THESE THREE CHANNELS:

Google Search. Google is by far the biggest ad platform. What makes it different is that people are already "searching" for a product like yours (imagine someone typing in "best natural deodorant"). This means they're more likely to complete a purchase from a Google Search ad than if they're, say, just scrolling Facebook and see an ad from you that they don't care about. This, combined with Google's comparatively low costs, makes it a slam dunk for many brands selling consumer products online. Google will also tell you about the keywords/SEO (search engine optimization) leading people to your brand (market research hack).

Facebook and Instagram. Ads here are often referred to as "paid social." People can have conversations about your products and engage with your brand directly, creating community. It's an opportunity to create a branded, visual experience. Facebook can be used to sell products effectively, but consider using it instead to drive engagement and awareness, rather than focusing 100 percent on converting sales. These costs are much lower than clicks, and you can get people introduced to/aware of your brand more efficiently.

Amazon. As of this writing, Amazon is now the third-largest ad platform, and if you're selling on Amazon, you need to explore advertising there. Think of it as a combo of Google and Facebook, where people are searching with the intent to purchase (they're ready to buy), but you can also provide more detailed product information and visuals.

Chris was a natural at marketing. He understood how to capture people's attention. Not long after Oliver was born, he'd started consulting for corporate clients in the media and sportswear industry, working in video and multimedia content creation. When there was something to learn—about SEO, for instance, or selling on Amazon—he'd pick up a book or spend hours in front of the computer and figure it out. I felt incredibly lucky and inspired to have him by my side. It seemed obvious that we should commit to him working for Schmidt's full time.

In April 2014, Chris officially joined forces with me. In addition to ads, he took over social media, content, the website, and media outreach. He became my one-man marketing and customer support team, working from a desk in our living room. There was no room to spare in the production space I was renting, and it was a luxury to have him at home to get a start on dinner and pick up Oliver from school.

We were giddy to be all in together; everything was still new and exciting with the business, and it felt like we were embarking on an adventure. I remember sharing my excitement on Facebook, announcing to the world that together, Chris and I were "in it to win it." From the work Chris had done so far, we were able to estimate how much profit we expected to generate through ads each month. We knew we weren't making enough to equate to two full salaries, but we could cover rent, childcare, food, and basic expenses. We trusted we'd be able to scale with our new strategy. And we did—within the first month, the results exceeded our expectations. After paying our bills, we funneled whatever profits were left back into online advertising, increasing our spend and revenue every month.

So you're working with your spouse

TIPS FOR RIDING THE ROLLER COASTER TOGETHER

Understand your own strengths and weaknesses.
In other words: don't micromanage. I knew Chris was exceptional in his areas of expertise, and I trusted him to take the reins, which freed me up to focus on what I needed to do on my end. We trusted each other to own our respective parts of the business and communicated constantly to keep each other in the loop.

Agree to disagree sometimes. Don't expect to be in perfect harmony 100 percent of the time. We generally agreed with each other but sometimes got stuck in the weeds on details. We learned to focus on where we *did* agree and to be patient enough to revisit some conversations later.

Be mindful of how your dynamic might impact others. When we hired one of our managers, she said, "I wish it had been disclosed to me before accepting the job that you two were married." Apparently, she'd had a bad experience in the past. We appreciated the feedback and started mentioning it in future interviews.

Take turns being the rock. When one is especially overwhelmed or under pressure, the other should listen, console, and support. This was a must for maintaining our sanity and connection.

Don't resist the overlap between work and life.
Embracing the way work and life were intertwined
worked for us. We knew it wouldn't be forever, and
more often than not, it was exciting. We maintained
boundaries, but didn't get too uptight if, say, we ended
up talking about Schmidt's at home after work.

For early ads, Chris used professional photos of the
deodorant paired with language highlighting our founding
story and what made us unique, as well as how we were being
received by recent press. Stuff like, "Made in a Portland, OR,
kitchen with natural, vegan ingredients and essential oils like
cedarwood and bergamot. Endorsed by Alicia Silverstone
and Fox!" I was meticulous about how our ads looked, and
Chris tested dozens of variants of images and copy at once
to see what was performing best. We were intentional about
every decision so that everything looked and sounded consistent. One carousel video ad was especially successful—
a sequence of images of the five deodorants, with bright
colors and swirling illustrations from the labels in the background that created a strobing, hypnotic effect. When the ad
took off, we put more budget into it.

Orders were pouring in, which quickly allowed us to
scale from spending a hundred dollars a day on ads to several
thousand. That may sound like a lot—and conceivably, you
could start with much less—but Chris spent enough to test a
bunch of ads across different audience groups, and we were
committed to driving awareness regardless of whether it con-
verted to sales. When right away the return on investment
was eight to ten times, we scaled to spend more. Facebook

ads were relatively new at the time, and people weren't yet tired of seeing them in their feeds. Plus, they were affordable. Chris also developed Google ads, which were equally successful. In fact, they eventually became so successful that Google contacted Chris because they noticed Schmidt's ads were top performers among those from direct-to-consumer startup brands, and they wanted to partner with Schmidt's on running strategic campaigns. Chris learned to use the resulting data from Facebook and Google for consumer insights and research, allowing us to hone our messaging and "brand voice"—the tone we struck in our content online— and tap into new audiences. Our social media following was booming, and we were getting tons of new subscribers to the newsletter.

Doing the ad math

IN MAKING DECISIONS ABOUT AD SPEND, BE SURE TO CONSIDER THESE VARIABLES

CPA (cost per acquisition). CPA is how much you're willing to spend on acquiring a customer. For example, let's say an average customer spends twenty-five dollars at checkout. How much can you spend on advertising and still break even? Let's put your costs into the equation. Say it costs you five dollars to make the products for that twenty-five-dollar order, plus another five dollars to ship. This would leave you with fifteen dollars left over to spend on advertising and still break even. Now, it's up to you to decide— are you willing to break even and spend that entire fifteen dollars if it means getting a new customer? Or should you set your baseline closer to ten dollars, ensuring that you walk away with at least five dollars profit from each sale? Both are viable approaches, but consider . . .

LTV (lifetime value). Look at reports to see how many purchases your average customer makes over time. Let's assume it's 2.5. All of a sudden, that fifteen dollars to acquire a new customer just got a lot more valuable, since you can expect them to buy your products again at a later date. Every business has different considerations at play, but generally, if you get a repeat customer—even if you're just breaking even—it's a win. And if your product is amazing, they'll be sure to tell their friends, leading to even more sales.

The efficiency of online sales was a change of pace from working with retailers and distributors, which was more time intensive: building the relationship, making the deal, shipping the product in bulk, waiting for transactions to occur, then waiting even longer for the money to finally come back. Our ads brought people straight to the website, where they'd buy deodorant directly. That influx of cash went back into improving operations, so we could keep up with demand. Plus, we could then contact these customers directly via email, incentivize them to purchase again, and encourage them to spread the word about Schmidt's on our social media channels.

In addition to everything Chris was doing on social media, he also helped expand on Mia's outreach strategy by organizing a big, unsolicited snail mailing of deodorant samples to as many major magazines as we could find addresses for. Our goal was to get featured in a big-name publication. We packed up dozens of unbranded white boxes (we didn't have custom ones yet) with multiple scents and a pitch letter, affixed a "Schmidt's" sticker on the front, and addressed most with "ATTN: BEAUTY EDITOR." We piled them into the trunk of my car and shipped them at the post office. Some were returned marked "undeliverable," but others arrived safely and resulted in a few "thank you" emails. Even if no one chose to feature Schmidt's, I knew we were still gaining valuable exposure just by getting on the radar of editors. One package sent to an editor from *Elle* led to Schmidt's appearing in its glossy pages a few months later. I was ecstatic. You don't always need a fancy plan or a pricey PR firm to get the job done.

Weigh the pros and cons of Amazon

In June 2014, with Chris leading the charge, we put two of our mid-performing products up for sale on Amazon to test out the platform (Cedarwood + Juniper and Ylang-Ylang + Calendula). We figured we'd see how they performed, knowing we'd still pick up sales on our top-performing sellers like Lavender + Sage and Bergamot + Lime on our website.

Collecting five-star reviews became a primary focus from the outset. Products with great reviews rank higher in searches and see higher conversion rates—that is, people are more likely to complete the purchase. As a result, we'd seed cards in our shipments that said "FIVE STARS," encouraging people to leave reviews or reach out to our customer support (which enabled us to address their concerns and also retain their email addresses). When customers did leave feedback in the reviews, we responded whenever possible. Commenting on everything, especially the negative, shows customers you're there and paying attention.

We also began advertising on Amazon and were impressed by the ads' performance—much like our Google ads, they were super successful because they were being seen by people who were already actively shopping.

But Amazon also posed huge challenges and became increasingly time-consuming for Chris to manage. Third-party sellers persisted on the site, often threatening the reputation of the brand by doing things like shipping items late, or packaging the product in scuffed, crappy, unbranded boxes. Worse yet, they regularly undercut our pricing. We implemented a Minimum Advertised Price (MAP) policy, which mandated that third parties buying Schmidt's could not sell the product below a certain price. Sellers still broke this policy, but it gave us reason to block them from buying Schmidt's in the future. Later, we hired outside agencies who specialized in managing third-party sellers, making sure they used approved photos and the appropriate claims, descriptions, and pricing.

Keeping up with ads, third-party sellers, and other such issues all made selling on Amazon time-consuming and frustrating. It became one of Chris's least favorite tasks. Still, we agreed our presence on the platform was worth it. I'd known from the very beginning that putting myself out there came with risks. I also knew, though, that I wasn't willing to forego the opportunity just because it was difficult. To this day, Chris and I agree that selling on Amazon has proven to be worthwhile, thanks to the accessibility it provides for our range of customers, the exposure gained, and the volume of sales made.

Does your order fulfillment process offer customers a good experience?

GET AND RETAIN CUSTOMERS BY OPTIMIZING YOUR SHIPPING PROCESS

Appearance. Up to 75 percent of people make repurchase decisions based on their original unboxing experience. When it comes to investing in packaging design, you can solicit bids from multiple vendors and choose the best and most cost-effective. Consider branding elements like bubble mailers, printed tape, tissue paper, and inserts with product instructions, your brand story, and feedback solicitation. When Schmidt's made packaging upgrades, we saw our retention spike.

Cost. When people abandon their carts at checkout, it's most likely due to the shipping fee. As such, incentivize with free shipping as much as possible, and compensate by raising the price of your product marginally.

Speed. Thanks to the normalization of two-day shipping, customers won't tolerate long shipping times. And if they do receive your product late, they're far less likely to reorder from you. To compete, a two-day turnaround time became our own policy/target for website orders. Later, Chris regularly met with and stress-tested the capabilities of our shipping and production teams to make sure we could accomplish our goal.

Join forces

In mid-2014, I received a curious email from someone named Kent Schmidt, of a famous Schmidt family in California, who said he and his business group wanted to discuss a "collaborative effort/private label." The email included short bios for each member of the group, which included Kent's sons Kendall, Kevin, and Kenneth, along with their business partner, Michael Cammarata. The introduction stated that Kendall was a famous singer-songwriter; Kevin was a reputable actor; and Michael was an innovative technological entrepreneur. The group was interested in "wholesome and healthy personal care products" to present to their retail contacts, Kent wrote. I wasn't sure what to make of the email. *Is this spam?*

The only way to find out was to respond. I asked to hear more, and Kent replied expressing further interest in developing some sort of mutually beneficial private label product line, adding that they had relationships with big-box stores and chain retailers. I still wasn't sure exactly what he had in mind, but my interest was piqued enough to set up a call and hear him out.

On the phone, Kent introduced himself and his son, Kevin, as owners of a conscious lifestyle brand they were interested in expanding through a potential partnership with me. They said they'd heard of Schmidt's through a contact at an essential oils supplier who'd asked them if they were related to the company, given the shared last name. The Schmidts had invested in retail businesses like mine before, Kent said, and their team had a connection to outlets like Costco, where they'd done business before. When

I heard "Costco," I perked up. Because we had the same last name, Kent pitched the idea of promoting Schmidt's to his family's networks, specifically among Kendall and Kevin's large fanbases, to our mutual benefit. He asked me about the kind of infrastructure I had in place and the amount of capital I thought I might need to meet a surge in demand (including filling a fifty-three-foot semi-trailer truck for Costco, ha ha), along with other questions about the current state of Schmidt's and its future.

I didn't have all the answers (and I wasn't sure how much I should tell them), but by the end of the call, I was curious enough to keep the conversation going. The pair seemed genuine and knowledgeable. And if they had the kind of access they claimed—to huge audiences of potential customers—that alone made me interested in learning more.

What followed was a series of calls and emails in which we continued to get to know one another and began exploring possible collaboration structures. Kent's son Kevin became my main point of contact, along with his business partner, Michael. The two wanted to assess what Schmidt's needed in order to scale, and they asked to see a balance sheet of the company's assets, profit and loss statements for the last two years, and a list of items needed for expansion and their associated costs. Naturally, I was hesitant to share too much, but I found a local attorney specializing in partnerships and acquisitions who became an important support system (and offered me a reduced rate as a small business owner), then proceeded with caution.

I used QuickBooks to generate reports and told the team what the business needed in the near future to meet growing demand, including a labeling machine, a bigger mixer, a pallet jack, and more staff. We discussed the phases of growth the company would need to undergo to be able to hit mass retail—to get on shelves in stores like Costco, CVS, and Target—and they explained how they could contribute. The plan included everything from getting new equipment, moving into a bigger warehouse/production space, acquiring special software, attending more expos, expanding PR efforts, leveraging celebrity endorsements, and so on.

My company had experienced so much organic, rapid success up to this point that I'd always felt secure and optimistic proceeding on my own. I knew I was already on a path to realizing my big vision of getting Schmidt's into the hands of as many people as possible. But my conversations with Kevin and Michael illuminated what was possible through working with them—including faster, more seamless access to massive opportunities and beyond—making me eager to explore the relationship.

Thanks to a surge in online sales from Chris's efforts and our growing list of retail accounts, Schmidt's was profitable (not always the case for a young stage company) and on pace to eclipse 2013's sales by about 500 percent—going from $132,000 to more than $600,000. We'd already outgrown our latest production space (thankfully, a vacancy next door allowed us to expand), but we were starting the process of hiring a few more employees to support shipping and were already beginning to run out of room yet again. All kinds of big challenges lay ahead of me: hiring, managing, and growing a team of employees, finding a professional production space along with industrial equipment that could support increasing demand, working with distributors, handling increasing international accounts and regulations—the list went on and on. I had confidence I could handle these growth challenges on my own, just as I'd done up to this point, but the idea of not having to do it alone was also appealing.

However, just as I was warming up to the idea, the discussion morphed from that of a private label or joint venture into talks about a more equitable partnership. When Kevin proposed equal share in the company—splitting it 50/50—Chris and I were immediately turned off. Additionally, they proposed that their side, which they later referred to as KM Organic Fund, would contribute "up to Thirty Eight Thousand Dollars ($38,000) worth of equipment, services, cash, or lines of credit." That amount would be helpful, but for a business arrangement like this, it wasn't very much. And to give up 50 percent of the company I'd built from my own kitchen? I couldn't imagine it. I pushed back, asking instead for a gradual buildup of equity over time, which felt much more comfortable. I wanted to know exactly how they imagined themselves being involved in decision-making for the business. I wasn't naive; I understood Schmidt's would probably represent only a small piece of their business efforts and attention, while of course for me it was everything. What kind of support would they provide, *exactly*, on a day-to-day basis? What would happen if they were unavailable? How was this whole thing going to work?

Kevin reassured me about the group's devotion to the company. I came back with more questions. He answered. This went on for months, until I agreed we should meet in person. In August, Kevin and Michael flew to Portland. For our first meeting, Kevin suggested lunch at a restaurant downtown along the river. Chris and I arrived early and waited outside. When we saw two men walking toward us wearing khakis and polo shirts, we knew it was them.

We took a seat at a table on the patio outside, under a clear, sunny sky. Kevin, an actor by trade, was chatty and friendly, exuding a warm, easygoing vibe. He did most of the talking, while Michael, more reserved, remained mostly quiet. Over the course of our conversation, I liked the impression I got. While Kevin and Michael were relatively new to the natural products category, that lack of knowledge felt okay to Chris and me because ours was so strong. Meanwhile, they spoke about the value they could bring to Schmidt's, especially when it came to connections, and presented a business sensibility that impressed me. Our areas of expertise complemented one another, and we shared the same ultimate goal of getting Schmidt's to as many people as possible.

After lunch, we all headed to the production space. I'd warned them ahead of time that it was a modest operation. Our "warehouse" was part of a small, one-story building that housed a few businesses (a pet shop, a paper shredding business, and us). We shared a restroom off the back hallway with the adjoining pet store, and a free-range turtle often spent his days hanging out in the hallway, so anyone who used the bathroom had to be careful not to step on him.

I introduced my guests to our small but mighty team: Ben, Alex, and Chris's mom, who came in occasionally to help with lids, labeling, and packing. (She actually enjoyed the work so much that she later become a full-time employee, and I was grateful to have her.) Alex worked in the back at the mixing and pouring station, while Ben, who now managed all aspects of shipping and helped with supply chain, worked from a desk in the front. Ben had recently become my first salaried employee. Around each employee and their respective station (and in my little office in the back corner), pallets, boxes of shea and cocoa butter, bottles of essential oils, and enormous bags of baking soda and arrowroot powder occupied every available space. On my desk were printouts about warehouses I had my eye on for my next move. As critical as our space needs were, it tended to go to the bottom of the priority pile, given all the other more pressing ones.

After showing Kevin and Michael around and introducing them to everybody, we parted ways for the afternoon. That night, we met at a cocktail bar downtown, where all of us could unwind and get to know one another a bit better. The conversation flowed smoothly, and I genuinely enjoyed our time together. It was reassuring that we could get along well, business aside. And it was clear that, if they followed through on their promises, they could help Schmidt's grow.

After the Portland visit, our correspondence continued over email. Meanwhile, I landed accounts with Pharmaca, Natural Grocers, and the Vitamin Shoppe (with potential to expand across more than seven hundred stores!), and I brought in a broker team in the Midwest who specifically targeted natural grocery chains and helped me pick up an account with Fresh Thyme, a huge natural food market. I devoted more and more of my time to managing our growing international presence, too, as I had to research how to meet the specific legal and testing standards required by each country. Thanks in part to the product's popularity in the blogger community, Schmidt's was in demand across the globe. To keep up, I hired two production and shipping assistants, Mike and Shaunee, who, like Alex, reported to Ben.

In September, I flew to LA for a pop-up event, and joined Kevin and Michael for another meal and long discussion.

Through it all, they stuck to their 50/50 offer. They said the only way they'd do business with us was if each party was equally invested. Anyone who's familiar with business investing knows that a $38,000 investment in a profitable company that is earning over $600,000 in revenue—and growing around 500 percent in a year—would typically not result in anything close to a 50/50 partnership. Chris and I were aware of how unusual their proposition was and were uneasy about it. Still, we knew Schmidt's had huge untapped potential, and felt the business would be poised to grow faster if we brought in the right people. With their backgrounds and expertise, it seemed like this partnership could help me avoid expensive mistakes and missteps, as well as assist in getting our finances in better order. Plus, the Schmidt family had been successful at making a name for themselves in the entertainment industry and brought with them a built-in fan base I was excited to expose my products to. After a lot of deliberation, I finally agreed to a 50/50 arrangement with KM Organic Fund. I knew it was a risk, but I was ready to trust my intuition, take a leap of faith, and seize the opportunity. After all—what was 50 percent, if we could potentially quadruple our business? Little did I know, we were about to do that, and then some.

By the end of the year, our tiny crew had made and sold $673,000 worth of deodorant, and I felt ready to shoot for the stars. Starting in the new year, I'd have the help of my new business partners. ■

What to make of it

 It's not about perfection; it's about showing up.

The Fox News opportunity challenged me on a deep level. But when the calls started coming in, along with a volume of orders like I'd never seen, I realized I'd done the right thing. Being an entrepreneur requires stepping out of your comfort zone—that's often where the big rewards lie.

 There's no growth without collaboration.

At the time the partnership deal was proposed, Schmidt's was growing quickly, thanks to my and Chris's efforts and those of our small team. But we saw the benefit of bringing in strategic support. It's hard for any entrepreneur to let go of control (or at least it was for me), but there comes a point when the benefit of welcoming new perspectives (through partnership, strategic hires, working with consultants, or whichever path is right for you) is more valuable than remaining closed off.

 Don't let fear of failure stop you in your tracks.

Every decision I made came with the risk that it could be the wrong choice. While the thought wasn't pleasant, I had to accept failure was possible and move forward anyway—there was no other way to grow. Each step I took to get to the next level required taking a risky leap, then trusting that I'd be able to figure things out.

CHAPTER 8

Be true to your intentions, flexible in your approach.

Hold fast to authenticity while remaining open to change.

Walking through the little 750-square-foot Schmidt's production space in early 2015, I had to navigate a maze of raw materials, packing supplies, and product. Even getting to and from my desk in my office was an obstacle course of countless boxes. Schmidt's was scaling rapidly—an exciting prospect, and certainly one I had hoped for, but not necessarily one for which I was prepared.

The Fox News segment was followed a few months later by a feature on the *Today Show*. Thankfully, I didn't need to appear on screen while Kathie Lee and Hoda took turns applying Schmidt's to their underarms, which was a relief. It wouldn't be much longer before talking to the press became a welcome part of my daily life, but for now, I was grateful to remain off camera.

Thanks in part to these big press moments, along with Chris's full-time dedication to marketing, and our continued presence in an increasing number of retail locations, Schmidt's continued to blow up—and it was still just the beginning. In the year ahead, we would experience a 550 percent increase in online sales, become the number one–selling deodorant on Amazon, and earn $2 million in revenue. Two *million*—an unfathomable number, one I never imagined I'd use in relation to my business. Such extreme scaling demanded I respond quickly to every opportunity, using them to continually think bigger—and then even bigger still. It required getting more help, satisfying more customers, investing in more machinery, and moving to a bigger warehouse (farewell, turtle). It meant expanding our content strategy, expertly managing a growing digital marketing budget, and getting many, many free samples of deodorant into the hands of the right people.

I had an ambitious vision for Schmidt's, but we were still operating as a small, local, fledgling company. With our partnership agreement signed, I was eager to start off 2015 with the support and different ways of thinking this relationship might bring.

But what would that support look like? In truth, I wasn't sure. I expected to continue to run and operate the business with Kevin and Michael available as sounding boards and advisors for decision-making and problem-solving. I anticipated they'd form important contacts and leverage existing connections to facilitate Schmidt's growth, as they'd promised, and that we'd use the modest funds they invested in the company to help us get that labeling machine.

Still, those expectations were a far cry from knowing what our day-to-day experience of working together would be like. How often would they come to Portland? How would we get aligned on big decisions for the business? We had a lot to learn. And just like in any relationship, I'd have to figure out when to compromise and when to stand my ground, how to communicate so that I'd be heard, and how to handle sticky situations as a team.

To help me navigate the change and growth that comes with working with others—and with all the progress in my business in the year to come—I developed a guiding principle: be true to your intentions and flexible in your approach. This kind of thinking came intuitively to me. I'd been through troubling times before (my divorce or dealing with my vocal condition) and had to find ways to cope and move forward. When things didn't feel perfectly under my control, or when the path seemed to be making unexpected turns, I'd try to take a high-level view and ask, *Am I still moving toward my big vision, even if the approach has changed or evolved?* If the answer was yes, then I felt securely aligned with my authentic purpose, even if things weren't exactly as I'd initially envisioned. I continually worked toward my goal of making healthy deodorant available to more people, which eventually became my stated ambition to be "the new face of natural"—a kind of natural that was modern, accessible, and effective. Remaining confident and aware of my own guiding principle allowed me to be open and expansive to new ideas.

Invest in a professional production floor and process

Long gone were the days of landing retail accounts by showing up at grocery stores with samples of deodorant in one arm and Oliver in the other. Chris now took on the task of pitching bigger accounts and chain stores, while my brokers Mia and Lisa continued their efforts, along with a few other brokers I'd hired for additional territories. Schmidt's was covering the map. Now my days were spent largely in front of my computer, processing myriad tasks: trying to keep track of who I needed to consider as a new partner, which existing accounts needed to be invoiced or were late on payment, which retailers needed a response to a special request, which orders to prioritize—it went on and on.

Thankfully, Ben had become a trusted keyman who made sure everything in production (or the "back of the house") ran smoothly while I stared at my inbox. He'd gone from packing boxes on Oliver's old diaper changing table in my garage to serving in a management role, overseeing many aspects of the business, from production, to supply chain, to shipping, to briefly helping out with customer support, and more. In January 2015, because of ever-increasing demand, I hired another part-time assistant to join Ben, Alex, Mike, and Shaunee.

It was also clear that we needed a larger space. Kevin and Michael came to Portland for a few days to help Chris and me hunt for a new space. We didn't find the right spot, but finally, in April, Chris and I found a new home for the business, a 5900-square-foot warehouse in a business park. It was our first legitimate production space: more than seven times the size of our current space. It felt *huge*. I was mostly excited about having loading docks for outgoing and incoming shipments. (When I'd attempted a pallet delivery at our previous space, it was too tight of a squeeze, and the door frame was torn apart. Oops.)

Moving into this space was a big moment. If our little office/production space/warehouse hadn't quite felt "official" before, it did now (though even as I ordered furniture and equipment, I still couldn't shake the feeling that I was playing house). The "front of the house" area included room for a conference table (our first!), a kitchen/break room furnished with a table and chairs from IKEA, a bathroom, and an office for me (Chris would continue to work from home and pick up Oliver/start dinner). I set up a water cooler delivery service and laundry service for towels and aprons (I'd been doing the wash myself), along with services for carpet vacuuming and cleaning the bathrooms and kitchen.

We positioned Ben's desk in an area between the front and back, and the rest of the warehouse space was dedicated to making and shipping deodorant. Ben drew up a production/shipping floor plan with AutoCAD (drafting and designing software), which was an enormous help. We needed to make sense of how to best arrange new machinery, staging, shipping, and labeling stations, plus shelving for inventory and supplies. With Ben's plan in place, we brought over our big industrial melting pot from the previous space and added a second one. We continued to use a small filling machine powered by a foot pedal, but labeling by hand was far too time consuming—a full-time job for two people.

We finally began our hunt for a labeling machine. Being mindful of budget, Kevin and I found a used one and had it shipped to our new warehouse. Much to everyone's dismay, it arrived malfunctioning and missing parts. We called every mechanic in the area, but none of them were willing to deal with this dinosaur of a machine. I'm naturally frugal, but when cutting corners didn't pay off—like with this dysfunctional used labeler—it was a lesson in the importance of investing money where it counts. We found someone to haul away the old labeler, enlisted help from our attorney to get a refund, and bought a new one.

At last I hired a much-needed bookkeeper, Darcy, to manage invoices and help me with retailer communications. I gave her a desk in the front of the office where she could also act as a point of contact for any walk-ins. We had real phones for the first time, and soon Darcy became a screener for incoming calls and customer support (a huge relief for Ben, who had been kind enough to help me out but was increasingly too busy with other tasks to handle calls). I added a few folks to Alex's crew, too, so we had more support with production and shipping.

When it came to big financial decisions, like signing a lease for the new space, buying equipment, and hiring more employees, I was doing it all on an as-needed basis to continue to meet demand. I didn't have formal projections for Schmidt's, but I knew the numbers looked good. The big retail accounts I'd landed, like PCC, Sprouts, and Whole Foods (along with dozens of smaller accounts), provided a steady stream of cash, and with Chris focused full time on marketing, our online sales were booming.

Expand your retail reach by working with distributors

When we landed Sprouts, an account with over three hundred grocery stores that Mia helped bring in, Schmidt's began working with a large distributor (one of the biggest in naturals) for the first time. Often, beginning a partnership with a distributor happens in tandem with getting a commitment from a big retail account. Otherwise, the distributor isn't eager to bring in your product and risk having it sit in inventory. Once Sprouts confirmed they wanted to bring in Schmidt's, we were able to secure the distributor partnership.

Working with a distributor would give us better access to retailers (remember when New Seasons didn't want to work with me until I was "in distribution"?), and the partnership was an important step for the business. Once we'd landed our first distributor, I began exploring relationships with many others I wanted to partner up with, and it wasn't long before we had a deal with all the big natural products distributors.

Working with distributors
TIPS FOR A SEAMLESS TRANSITION

Research which one will make a good partner. Talk to key retailers to find out which distributors they prefer to work with, and get to know which ones specialize in your industry. Industry trade shows are a perfect place to meet potential distributors.

Prepare your product. Make sure you can meet production demands. Different distributors will have different requirements for shipping specs—for example, you may need to have custom boxes made. Labels must comply with legal requirements and have working barcodes.

Do the math. Working with a distributor will cut into your profit margins. Each will have their own standard, like a price that's 5 percent lower than your wholesale price, for example. Know what number you're comfortable agreeing to and don't be afraid to negotiate.

Ask distributors about promotional opportunities. These can result in an immediate boost in sales with the retailers your distributors are selling to.

Expect bumps along the way

In the midst of all the expansion that was taking place in Portland, I was experiencing mixed feelings about working with new partners. For the most part, business continued as usual, and I had the relative freedom to run my company the way I wanted while keeping my partners looped in, without much direct involvement from them for the time being. In our plans for this first phase of growth together, the focus was to get Schmidt's to a place where we could fill larger orders, and that responsibility fell to me. I was content to continue to manage that growth while trusting Kevin and Michael would do their part—facilitating connections—when the time came. (In retrospect, I put too much emphasis on the "trust" part of our relationship when I wish I would have put more in writing.)

Partnership did come with growing pains, and I felt them most when it came to decision-making. Now that I was a shared owner of the business, significant decisions required collective agreement to move forward. I had independence when it came to staffing and day-to-day operations, but I had to get their approval on other kinds of decisions, like determining whether to offer a special price to a retailer, or give a pay raise to an employee. My to-do list was long, and it was enormously frustrating to me when it took a couple days (or longer) to get a response. I'd always relied on moving quickly as a way of staying ahead of the competition and seizing opportunities. In working with partners—who weren't here in the office with me and who had other things going on—would I lose my edge? Was Schmidt's a high enough priority for them? Sometimes I wasn't sure. That spring, I'd flown to LA and attended the Natural Products Expo with Kevin, which had been productive and left me feeling more in sync with him. While Kevin made himself fairly available to me, though, Michael could be difficult to track down. When I suggested we begin scheduling a weekly check-in with the three of us, Michael replied that if I wanted to get in touch with him, I should put "URGENT" in the subject line of my email. To me, it was all urgent; Schmidt's was a growing business. In retrospect, it would have made sense to lay out our communication expectations up front.

One day in May, shortly after we moved into the big production space, Michael and I were on the phone running through my usual long list of topics for discussion, like what kind of special pricing we should approve for a new distributor in Australia or how many thousands of jars we were comfortable committing to on this PO. Our new distributor was hosting an upcoming trade show in Hawaii. It seemed like a hefty expense, but we agreed we should attend the show to get in good with our new partner. Besides, it was Hawaii, and Chris planned to come, too.

We were discussing all this when Michael dropped a surprising bomb—he nonchalantly mentioned that Kevin was no longer going to be involved in our work. He was out.

Though very confused, I didn't push (an approach I would learn was not the smartest). We rarely had an opportunity to connect to talk about the business, and we still had a lot more ground to cover, so we moved on to the next topic. Almost without even realizing it, I let it drop. We were about to have our first business trip together, and I wanted it to go smoothly. I didn't have time to dwell on the news.

Before you partner up
HINDSIGHT IS 20/20. WHAT TO CONSIDER BEFORE GOING INTO BUSINESS WITH SOMEONE

Research and reference. Trusting your gut is important, but so is doing your due diligence, like talking to other professionals who have worked with the person you are potentially bringing into a business. Internet scrubbing is a thing, so these one-on-one conversations can be more meaningful to your research than Google.

Put it all in writing. Your titles, salaries, and job descriptions. Have a candid conversation about values and principles, as well as your company's history and story, and put all that into writing, too.

Look at the long view. No one can predict the future, but it's critical to discuss a long-term vision for the company, including growth channels, potential exit strategies, bringing on additional partners, etc.

Don't accept anything as impossible

While all this was happening—the big move, the new hires, the never-ending onslaught of emails, and the adjustments in my new partnership—I had another massive task on my to-do list: it was time to get back in the kitchen and formulate a stick version of Schmidt's. I had been working on adding it to our lineup since 2012, but now it was a bigger priority than ever in order to compete with the larger players. A stick option was sure to be a huge hit with our customers and a milestone for the company.

From the early days of running the business, I recognized that a jar was not only the best container for my formula, it was also a significant differentiator for the brand. It was unusual to find deodorant in any form other than a stick, and while the jar confused and surprised people at first, it also got their attention. The jars made us recognizable; they distinguished us from the sea of options, and they were a selling point. Plus, the sustainability and aesthetic appeal of the glass had always been a benefit.

All that said, from day one, customers wanted a stick version. I knew some jar loyalists would convert to the stick if offered, and that it would expand our market significantly, reaching people who just didn't want to use their hands or add extra time to their routine while trying to rush out the door in the morning. Knowing I'd reach more people with a stick version, I could be true to my intention (sharing Schmidt's widely) and flexible in my approach (open to a new formula and form).

There was just one problem. I'd been trying to formulate a stick version for years and hadn't been able to nail the formula. I continued to put it off to focus on other (easier) executive priorities, but now that the brand had so much momentum, it was time to take the challenge head-on. It was an enormous undertaking to reformulate my perfectly crafted recipe to give it the consistency necessary for a stick, while being effective like the jar formula, and using only natural ingredients. Most traditional deodorants contain synthetic additives like propylene glycol (an ingredient that facilitates glide), which I'd never use. Unwilling to adjust my standards, I had to find my own way.

I returned to my "mad scientist" days of formulating at home. I worked from my kitchen where it was easiest to make countless iterations in small batches (at the warehouse, our equipment was dedicated to larger-scale manufacturing). The task at hand required a change in the ratio of ingredients, as well as the introduction of new ones in order to achieve an effective glide. It was a painstaking process of isolating one variable at a time, making the batch, testing various cooling and setting times, and then waiting to see how the final product came together (Was it too dry? Too hard? Too grainy? Too soft?), and then how it performed on humans. I tried many ingredients I didn't end up using—aloe, witch hazel, a variety of clays, and milk of magnesia. With each batch, I analyzed and drew conclusions about how an ingredient or process impacted the formula. It had to be perfect—this time I wouldn't have the luxury of taking a handful of products to the farmers market for feedback, then tweaking it; I'd (hopefully) be immediately shipping thousands to customers and retailers nationwide.

I created countless iterations, slowly getting closer. Multiple times I thought I'd pulled it off, but after the product had a couple days to settle, some formulations would dry out or become crumbly or mushy, meaning it wasn't shelf stable and certainly wouldn't function properly. At one point, I called a chemist for help. She explained that a smooth texture would be difficult to create, as the baking soda and arrowroot powders have a tendency to want to clump back together.

"How can I fix that?" I asked.

"I'm not sure you can," she said, and suggested a synthetic binder, which for me was not an option. I was determined to keep trying the way I had been, steadily adjusting mixing times and melting temperatures, using only the ingredients I believed in. I'd come this far and had to have faith I could get to the finish line. This business was my livelihood, in every sense of the word. I couldn't let anything—not fears, not fatigue, not negative assumptions—get in the way.

With each batch, I'd swipe the deodorant on my own underarms and leave for work. I'd test it for days, and if it seemed to be working, I'd keep going, tracking its performance for a week or so. I re-recruited Chris for testing, too.

Any unwanted body odor was unacceptable, and we would laugh when I would walk up to him and dig my nose into his underarm throughout the day, just as I had when developing my first formula. When a formula failed, I went back into the kitchen that much more determined to get it right. Halfway into 2015, I was getting a lot closer. I was making smaller and smaller adjustments to a promising formula. One day at the office, I realized I'd been using the latest formulation for a week—and it was doing the job. It was easy to apply, stable, glided smoothly, and most importantly, it worked.

"This is the one!" I told Chris and Oliver when I walked in the door. I'd done it. It was time to introduce this new member of the Schmidt's family to the world. I couldn't wait.

Launch with a bang

While I'd been formulating the stick and overseeing production, retail accounts, and everything in between, Chris was taking the Schmidt's brand to the next level online. From our tiny living room, he'd grown our Facebook following from two thousand to one hundred thousand, established us as a top-selling deodorant on Amazon, and continued to lock in our reputation as a natural deodorant that actually worked. What's more, he was helping us take a more ambitious approach to content, releasing a steady stream of videos and product photos that featured our formula and scents, our customers, and my founding story. Our messaging often incorporated phrases like "change the way you think about natural" or "we're taking natural to the next level" to help position Schmidt's as a differentiator and disruptor in the space. I loved weighing in on creative decisions and collaborating with Chris on different kinds of content;

we shared the same tastes and both enjoyed the artistry of the work. We aslo knew that by positioning ourselves as a modern, unconventional player in the category, we would stand out from our competition.

We also knew the stick launch would be a pivotal moment for the company. Even before I nailed the final formula, we began planning how to pitch press, launch social media campaigns, spread the word, and get equipped to manufacture this new product, which would require additional machinery, processes, and staff. In late spring, we began a months-long effort to get ready, planning to first launch the product online and to select retailers by the end of summer, followed by a big announcement to all retailers in the fall.

I went back to the same design firm that had created our jar labels and had them create new front and back labels for the sticks. Compared to the jars, the stick labels were much bigger, and I loved seeing how our design took shape on them, especially compared to the cluttered, conventional styles of many of my competitors. Once the labels were complete, Chris scheduled a photo shoot, and we updated our lookbook for retailers, bloggers, and members of the press. It was a fashion-industry approach to branding that helped us stand out. We also planned to use the new photos in revamped line sheets, in ads, on our own website, and across marketing channels. In advance of launching, Chris created inactive listings on Shopify, Etsy, and Amazon that would go live at launch, and he updated our advertising and SEO strategy across outlets. We designed custom shipping boxes for retailers to accommodate the new sticks (which had the Schmidt's logo printed on each side), as well as custom-designed shelf boxes that could sit directly on store shelves and show off our new products (for a subset of retail accounts that displayed products this way).

We readied the manufacturing area and prepared to make thousands of sticks, which we planned to launch in all five scents. One mixing vat would be dedicated to jar production and the other to sticks. I hired several additional staff members for the production team. We ordered a filling machine and a labeler specifically for stick production, but unfortunately the machines would require six to twelve weeks of assembly time before being shipped to us. In the meantime, the team would need to fill and label each stick by hand—a time-consuming process.

Production did not go smoothly from the outset. I'd perfected my formula in a pot on the stovetop, and I quickly discovered that making it in mass quantities was a whole new ballgame. Initial batches had all kinds of issues: the butters and powders separated, they dried lumpy, or the glide factor just wasn't there. I worked closely with Alex (who continued to be my steadfast production lead) to make adjustment after adjustment until every stick came out just right.

In the months before the planned September launch, Chris began pitching press, while Darcy and I culled our retail list and identified which ones had a category reset deadline approaching. To those and to other select accounts, I sent an email announcement about the exciting new launch. I scheduled a few in-store meetings with buyers, too, and sent samples to large chains.

As launch approached, Chris directed Ben's team to mail samples to two hundred select media influencers and past supporters of the brand. Our production team worked to produce a backlog of inventory so we'd be prepared when orders started to hit. We wanted to be sure to have close to ten thousand on hand, especially because we knew customers had high expectations for fast shipping. We also wanted to make the sticks available on the Amazon store at launch, so we prepared a massive amount for Amazon's fulfillment centers.

Producing all this deodorant wasn't easy, especially because in the process of pitching press, we'd landed a big opportunity with *Allure*, who'd invited us to submit twenty-four thousand travel-size samples of jar deodorant for inclusion in their subscription beauty box. We needed to get that massive order out the door right at the same time the sticks were set to become available. Each mini jar had to be labeled by hand, meaning that on some days, up to three employees did nothing but label for our *Allure* order (instead of working on stick production). And the filling and labeling machines we'd ordered months before had yet to arrive.

In early September, with our ten thousand sticks finally at the ready and our *Allure* order well in development, we launched. First, the sticks went live exclusively on the website, supported by a newsletter announcement and a big social media push. Our messaging told the story of how hard I had worked to develop the deodorant, positioning Schmidt's as having "cracked the code" of an effective natural deodorant you could now apply with a familiar stick. In addition to sharing the story of my kitchen-made recipe, we always emphasized our one-of-a-kind scents. We also underscored—as we had from the beginning—that our formula *worked*, and was now easier to use. Our biggest seller? A new "Deluxe Five-Pack" box set, allowing customers to try each of our scents, or share with friends.

We gave away hundreds of products to influencers, bloggers, writers, and editors. Chris tracked every engagement, from unanswered emails to press features. It seemed like every week, a new "green beauty" blog or YouTube sensation popped up on our radar, and we'd try to get our product into their hands. When successful, that boosted our reputation and rapport everywhere. The buzz on social media, blogs, and YouTube was beyond what we expected. We immediately picked up new Schmidt's users who had been interested in Schmidt's but reluctant to try the jars. It was a celebratory moment for the brand, and for me personally.

Launch it
A SAMPLE MARKETING CHECKLIST FOR NEW PRODUCT ROLLOUTS

One to two months before launch

- Let select bloggers, supporters, and buyers preview samples at trade shows and via mail (prioritize big accounts and those with time-sensitive category resets)

- Update advertising strategy (keywords, ad campaigns, social campaigns) and SEO

- Prepare blog posts and educational materials to introduce your products

- Create an FAQ to prepare your customer support department and train them on the answers

- Create teaser customer newsletter and social posts to release about one to two weeks before launch

- Create inactive listings on your website, Amazon, etc.

- Prepare launch-specific ads for launch day

- Pitch magazines, press outlets, influencers, etc., targeting existing contacts

- Send retailer-specific announcements about four to six weeks before accepting orders

- In the days before launch, leak product to select influencers and top customers

Launch day

- Product goes live across all platforms

- Send newsletters to customers, retailers, and partners

- Announce on social media and activate advertising

- Have customer support lined up to work after hours for the expected uptick in emails and calls

- Post blog content

- Stand by and watch the excitement!

Post-launch

- Product goes live on other platforms (depending on your strategy)

- Follow up with all media pitches

- Send retailer-specific announcements to accept retail orders

- Analyze ad campaigns based on performance and audience learnings (e.g., age, income, etc.)

and optimize by turning off ones that don't work, increasing budget for ones that do, adding more layers (e.g., location, age, gender) for ad sets that are "almost" working, etc.

- Do giveaways, etc.

Define your customer suppport values (and set the bar high)

When we launched the stick, I wanted people to love the product as much as I did, and if they weren't satisfied, I wanted to fix it. My return policy had always been generous. Sometimes that meant sending a replacement or a different scent. Sometimes that meant spending precious time on the phone, asking questions about a customer's experience and finding out what was causing dissatisfaction. This was always very important to me, and once I began assigning other employees to help with calls, I would explain my expectations around maintaining patience and empathy with every customer. This is a value that carried forward throughout our growth, and it remains an important tenet of our customer support team today.

Oftentimes I hear early-stage business owners say they're resistant to giving away their product for free. I understand the hesitation. But Schmidt's became known for excellent customer support, and it paid off. When we sent a disgruntled customer a new deodorant, we usually won them over, and, based on average deodorant usage, we knew that in three months' time they'd be back at the store buying Schmidt's (we always thought in terms of a customer's lifetime value). We considered it a marketing expense, like paying for an ad, but even more targeted, more effective, and—best of all—a little more personal. Plus, a generous return policy is simply good PR.

With the launch of the stick, we were aware we might disappoint jar enthusiasts who loved the sustainability factor of the recyclable, sustainable glass containers. In anticipation, we were excited to develop Schmidt's Recycling Club, a loyalty program where customers could mail five empty jars to us (to be cleaned and reused) in exchange for a free jar of deodorant. Even though the sticks were such a success (early sales numbers showed them outselling the jars eight to one), I knew I'd never stop offering the jars. They stood out on shelves, they were sustainable, and many customers still favored that style of application—and the product overall. From an economic standpoint, it wasn't costing the business much to continue offering them; the research and development was already done, the listings were on the website, the customers were loyal, and we had the equipment and trained staff to sustain it.

Customer relations— nothing is more important
KEEP HIGH STANDARDS

Replace. Whenever possible, send unhappy customers a replacement at no cost. If I thought I could retain a customer with a replacement, I viewed it as worth it. And if a refund was the best option, I did that.

Go above and beyond. Show there's a human side to the business. When the occasional customer complained Schmidt's left a stain on their shirt, I told them to send the clothing to me, and I would personally clean it. Customers were genuinely surprised, and it helped create loyalty. Eventually I had to stop hand-washing shirts, but my liberal exchange policy still stands.

Educate. Develop content that educates customers about your ingredients, process, policies, etc., from guides to videos to blog posts. We made an FAQ with questions like, "What's the difference between your sticks and jars?" and "Does Schmidt's contain aluminum?" to make it easy for customers to find answers.

Consider the long view. A lot of early-stage businesses struggle with justifying the costs of returns, exchanges, etc. My advice? Bite the bullet. Consider the lifetime value of a customer you keep: How much might they spend with you in the future if you take care of them the first time? And how many other customers might they introduce to your brand?

Bottom line: whenever you can, fix it. Experience taught me the value of word of mouth. I believe that a customer with a great experience will tell ten people. A customer with a bad experience will tell twenty. And a customer who had a bad experience that you fixed will tell fifty.

After the successful launch of the stick in September, I attended my first Natural Products Expo (one of the largest gatherings for natural and organic brands in the industry), in the hopes of landing more retail accounts. I'd been attending larger and larger trade shows as Schmidt's grew, but expos like this were a whole other level. I was stubbornly frugal and couldn't resist thinking about the cost of this (and everything in my life) in terms of how many deodorants I'd have to sell to cover it.

The following month, Michael came to Portland for a strategy meeting with Chris and me. The more he recognized the big moves the Schmidt's team was making, the more engaged he became. There was a lot to discuss. Even though we'd practically just moved in, we were rapidly outgrowing our latest production space. We were so overwhelmed with stick orders that we needed to postpone launching the new product overseas. Our filling and labeling machines were still MIA. There were holiday bonuses to talk about, the new PR firm we had just hired, marketing commercials, insurance policies, inventory reports, partnership opportunities, staffing plans, product development ideas, and much more. Schmidt's was on the verge of producing more deodorant than my eyes had ever seen. ∎

What to make of it

 ### Sometimes it pays to power through.

There were a few moments in the early days of my partnership when a feeling of panic washed over me—did I just make a huge mistake giving up half of my business? But Schmidt's was thriving, I was still inspired, and failure wasn't an option. I still had the power to come to work each day and be true to my intentions, flexible in my approach—however uncomfortable that was at times. Growing a business means leaning into your creativity and determination.

 ### Keep evolving your brand.

By 2015, the natural deodorant landscape had changed from when I'd first started out. Consumers had evolved, and so my messaging needed to as well to position Schmidt's as "the new face of natural." Staying tuned in to customers meant my strategy remained relevant and resonant.

 ### You can't please everybody.

When we launched our stick formula in plastic containers, I expected some pushback, even though the containers were partially composed of recycled plastic and were recyclable at certain locations. But the decision to move forward was best for the business and for many (if not most) of our customers. I wanted all our customers to feel considered, which is why our recycling program was so important.

CHAPTER 9

Maintain momentum.

Continue experimenting while learning to juggle growth, change, and inevitable challenges.

I n January 2016, I flew to Whole Foods' Southern California office for a meeting to discuss expanding our placement, as well as adding our new stick deodorant. Though I'd landed the Pacific Northwest and a few other regions pretty seamlessly, it was a bigger challenge to win a chain-wide placement—a spot on *every* Whole Foods shelf, an opportunity for which I'd just submitted a huge proposal. After all the hustle of 2015, the company had grown so much so quickly. I identified national placement in Whole Foods as the ideal next step, both in terms of being a great home for Schmidt's, and for opening the door to additional opportunities. One of my brokers helped facilitate the proposal submission, which required me to fill out a detailed spreadsheet with product information (from selling attributes to product dimensions) and build a presentation according to Whole Foods' guidelines. It wasn't a difficult process, but it was a tedious one.

However, soon after my return from California, I found out we hadn't been chosen for increased regional placement—or for the global opportunity either. Instead, Whole Foods had gone with a competitor I was very sensitive about—that same one customers had always compared Schmidt's to at markets, and one it seemed to me had been inspired by Schmidt's scents, formulations, and designs. To top it off, I found out part of the reason we failed to get the global placement was because I hadn't properly submitted our paperwork.

Whole Foods was an obvious opportunity we needed to land in order to sustain our growth and to demonstrate our rightful place as a leading natural deodorant. If we couldn't get Whole Foods, how were we going to claim ourselves as the top natural brand and get into other big retailers like Target, Walmart, and Costco? Back in Portland, we'd moved into a significantly larger warehouse across the corporate park and had continued to scale rapidly, but not without hiccups (which by now I'd come to expect, given the rapid pace of growth). Hiccups were signs of progress, I told myself. The labeling and filling machines, after a long seven months in production, had finally arrived in good order, and my employees were being trained on how to operate them safely. We could now produce several thousand units of deodorant in a day—but when our printing vendor kept delivering spools of labels with missing or illegible text, we faced serious delays. We'd also been dealing with an influx of customer complaints about faulty stick deodorant dials; they were getting stuck and not advancing upwards, rendering the product unusable. Getting to the root of the issue required a time-intensive deep dive into our manufacturing techniques and supply chain: Was it something with the sticks themselves? Was it the way we were filling them? Was it the cold temperatures in the warehouse? We still hadn't gotten to the bottom of it, and the issue persisted for much longer than I would have liked.

"Jaime, we have a problem," was a phrase I grew to expect at least once a day, and I didn't always have the answers. Issues ranged from a late delivery of raw materials, to a malfunctioning machine, to an upset customer. We now employed twenty people, and I felt personally responsible for keeping up our momentum, finding solutions for every issue, and leading us forward. The pressure was immense. Sometimes I looked around the warehouse and felt like I was hallucinating. *How had I come this far? And could I continue to keep up?* With popularity comes risk of losing your status. The stakes were higher than ever.

Even on a personal level, Schmidt's financial growth had become a double-edged sword. Despite our successes, my and Chris's finances were still unpredictable. The partnership agreement stipulated that for every quarter, each owner would take 25 percent of net earnings and 50 percent would remain in the business (it wasn't until later that we had salaries, which provided more predictability). In 2016 there were some quarters where we didn't give ourselves anything; sometimes we chose to keep all the money in the business, or the expenses were so high there was no money to be taken.

One morning I woke up, checked my phone groggy-eyed in bed, and saw an email from my accountant that I owed around $300,000 in personal income taxes. As the owner of the business, I had to pay taxes on earnings I wasn't necessarily bringing home. Even though Schmidt's revenues were higher than ever, almost all the money coming in went right back out in operating expenses, so at times our margin of profit was slim. In other words: I simply did not have the money to pay this tax bill. I filed for an extension and prayed everything would go smoothly as Schmidt's expanded. This kind of risk was unbearable if I stopped to dwell on it, but I knew if I could just tolerate it for the time being, we'd get to the other side. Our projections were solid; I needed to hustle to keep them that way.

Pitch it like you mean it

I didn't have time to wallow in the disappointment of Whole Foods, because another huge meeting was coming up in March, with Target (yes, *Target*). The year before, I'd met a representative of the brand at the Natural Products Expo. I was standing alone at our booth when the Target broker approached. He was already familiar with Schmidt's and told me directly he thought my product was a perfect fit for the store. After the event, we had a few follow-up calls; he introduced me to the buyer, and now, months later, it was time to fly to Minneapolis to formally present ourselves.

Tricks of the trade show (when you've got money to spend)

THOSE EARLY TRICKS OF THE TRADE SHOW FROM CHAPTER 6 ARE STILL RELEVANT, BUT WITH A HIGHER BUDGET, YOU CAN DO MORE.

Pay to promote. Blast Instagram, Twitter, and Google ads within a mile of the convention center. We used messaging tailored to attendees, including information like our booth number. Impressions could be worth a thousand times that of a normal customer (it could be a Target buyer seeing the ad), so we invested accordingly.

Bring a beautifully designed booth. We upgraded the sophistication of our booth design and hyped it on social media. We had backlit wall panels, a comfy couch with branded charging stations, floor graphics that incorporated our packaging illustrations, a sampling station, a place to sit and write orders, etc. Beyond splashing drab event halls with color, lighting goes a long way.

In our initial email conversations, the Target buyer suggested a few product updates he needed to see before potentially deeming Schmidt's ready for their shelves. For one, he thought our deodorant stick should be rounded at the top. Currently we were filling the sticks from the top, and the product would cool with a flat top before we capped them. He thought a rounded top would better suit customers' armpits. I had no idea what that would require—a major adjustment to our filling machine? Different stick containers? Nonetheless, naturally, I said, "Yes, we can do that."

He also asked us to include artwork on the caps. Our labels at the time were applied to the stick body, while the cap remained plain white. I wasn't sure how much of a challenge it would be to apply labels to the caps, too, but I said, "Yep, of course we can do that."

To show him we were serious, I bought little dome caps and hand-filled a few of our existing stick containers so they'd dry with rounded tops. Then I worked with our design team to quickly create artwork for the caps. I sent Target photos of our new-and-improved product and planned to bring the samples to the meeting.

Lastly, when it came to pricing, Target had specific requirements. Our $8.99 price point was too high for stores, they said, and they asked if we could come down much lower. To meet their request but still ensure it would be cost effective for us, we proposed a smaller deodorant stick than we sold at other retailers. The container would remain the same shape but would be shorter and filled with less product, 2.65 ounces versus 3.25 ounces. This smaller size was an industry standard and the same size as most conventional brands. We agreed that it was a solid and strategic decision for Schmidt's, but we knew it would require us to almost double the number of products we'd be producing—adding a whole new size for each scent meant a different label design, building out a separate space in the warehouse for storing them to avoid confusion, and giving them dedicated time on our manufacturing line.

Even though Target's requests would require costly changes to our production process, we knew it would be worth it. This was *Target* we were talking about. We agreed to their asks and prepared for the big meeting.

By now, I'd been to a couple dozen meetings like this for chain grocery stores and knew the drill. Typically, we only got about thirty minutes to present. It always went by in a flash: we were in and then out. Then there would be weeks— or even months—of waiting to hear the verdict. I always researched who would be in the room ahead of time, and the broker would give me a heads-up on the best strategy for approaching the specific retailer. I worked closely with Chris to develop a colorful and compelling presentation that was specific to each buyer. Over time, I developed a confident presentation and flow, starting with the company's story, walking through our products, highlighting incentives and promo support we had to offer, and making a case with data that showed why we belonged on their shelves.

Ever since the Fox News appearance, I'd taken my vocal condition more seriously. A few months after the spot aired, I'd found a specialist I trusted in Portland, and he recommended I try Botox treatments—right into my vocal cords. Because spasmodic dysphonia causes the muscles in the larynx to spasm, Botox injections are the only known treatments that can successfully relax the muscles and improve the condition. It doesn't work for everyone, but I was relieved and hopeful when, after my first treatment, my voice was noticeably smoother. Ever since that first injection, I'd worked closely with my doctor to find out how often I needed to schedule the treatment to maintain a "good" voice. After each treatment, I'd experience an initial period when my voice was very soft, followed by a period when it became stronger and smoother. Gradually the effect would wear off, and I'd return for treatment. It wasn't necessarily pleasant to be injected in the neck with a big needle every few months, but the effects meant everything. I had my voice back. And that meant I could walk into a meeting with Target with confidence. I continue to depend on this method of treatment to this day. Bringing awareness to the condition and supporting research into new treatment options has become one of my passions.

When Michael and I arrived in Minneapolis (which in and of itself was a feat; our initial flight from Portland was canceled, so we caught a last-minute train to Seattle and flew out from there—there was no way we were missing this meeting), we arrived at Target's office and were shown to a small waiting room. The buyer must have had back-to-back appointments, because right before we went into the board room, employees from Procter & Gamble, owners of Secret and Old Spice, two of the biggest names in deodorant, walked out. I smiled, wondering if they might recognize me as the Schmidt from Schmidt's Deodorant.

Once the meeting was underway in the tiny room, I told the story of the evolution of Schmidt's from my kitchen, then walked through our brand's value proposition, Target-specific marketing plan, consumer insights, and sales statistics from other stores to demonstrate how well Schmidt's was selling. We'd begun using a sales reporting database called SPINS, and I cited data indicating how well Schmidt's was performing among competitors in the naturals category.

Whenever I told the story of how I'd formulated Schmidt's at home, I could see buyers' eyes light up. Sometimes they'd stop me midway through to ask questions about my product's origins, and it was obvious my story was much different from the ones they were used to hearing. Customers appreciated knowing the deodorant came from humble origins and that the company's values could be trusted, but in meetings like this, it was exciting to see that my founding story also carried weight in the eyes of retailers: it communicated differentiation and authenticity for the brand.

The Target rep liked the new samples and generally seemed impressed. We left the meeting feeling hopeful. Now it was a waiting game.

Landing the deal
STRATEGIES FOR GETTING A LEG UP IN BUYER MEETINGS

Remember, *you* are the product expert. Instead of being intimidated by someone in a buying role, remember you're the expert on your product. Besides, these are just people like anyone else (fast-forward a couple years to when this same Target buyer messaged me on LinkedIn asking about a job at Schmidt's).

It's a conversation, not a pitch. Don't go in thinking you have to sell. Instead, approach the meeting as a conversation about why you make the products you make. Storytelling and authenticity win out over the hard sell every time.

But *do* be prepared to show how you can add value. Know your competitors—specifically what's on shelves at a given store—and speak to how you're creating new opportunities and bringing in new customers. Learn the buyer's key motivations and speak to them.

Make teamwork work

Back at the warehouse, in our new, bigger space, Chris, Michael, and I each had our own office. I'd helped Michael find an apartment in Portland that summer, so he didn't need to stay at a hotel when he was on-site. He was now spending several days a month in Portland, which was a nice change of pace from the days when he could be hard to track down on the phone. We had cubicles installed that would be filled by our new customer support manager and employees and Chris's growing marketing team (after the stick launch, we hired several new employees). We brought in a reception-ist/customer support person to allow Darcy to focus solely on bookkeeping and account management. We also hired several more employees to the production team. With our numbers growing, I set up human resources support services through an outside vendor. I wanted to be sure my paperwork was in order, establish job descriptions and a performance review process, and provide standard practice trainings on topics like harassment in the workplace and how to access benefits. I knew all these things were critically important, and with everything else I was juggling as CEO, it provided some peace of mind to have attention on this aspect of the business. Soon after, I added an in-house human resources manager and assistant, but for the time being, the outside agency helped.

With Chris now working in the office, we were spending nearly all of our time together. We'd take Oliver to the bus stop in the morning, then drive to work, determined to test out every possible Portland coffee shop that was within a reasonable distance of our office. At the end of the school day, we'd leave to pick up Oli, then continue working from home, juggling dinner (frequently from the Postmates delivery service), maintaining our home, and spending as much time with Oli as possible. Sometimes Chris's mom helped out if it was a day we both needed to be at the office or take a late meeting. That summer my sister-in-law Mady started babysitting for us, and Oliver loved working on DIY projects and going on little adventures around Portland with her.

It might sound crazy, but for the most part, Chris and I loved working side by side. It's important for me to have alone time to "reset," but living and breathing Schmidt's was exhilarating. We felt like a tight-knit unit, taking on the world together. And if anybody questioned us working together, Chris and I both would own it; it never bothered us.

I knew what an asset he was to the company, and also that he was legitimately proud of me and who I had become. It helped that we filled such different capacities, and also that Chris was progressive and confident enough to see the value in emphasizing my role as a female entrepreneur.

Not everything was seamless. At times when Chris or I wanted to offer a promotion or raise to members of our team, or bring on a new hire, getting Michael to agree to it was sometimes a struggle—and as partners, we both had to approve these things. While I understood the mentality of being frugal as a young company, I also knew that it ultimately cost more to have good people leave and need to recruit to fill their shoes, and that it could hurt us to not invest in strategic hires in the first place.

Despite our disagreements, the majority of the time we were on the same page. Especially for the period of time Michael was living partially in Portland, he, Chris, and I were in sync, working together toward a common goal.

Expand your product line strategically

I soon found myself back in the kitchen again, this time working on a sensitive skin version of the deodorant. A huge percentage of people purchasing personal care products identify as having sensitive skin, and I knew from my own customers that some experienced irritation from natural deodorant. Sometimes they simply needed to go through an adjustment period of getting used to the new product, and irritation would clear up after a few days, while others suspected a possible intolerance to baking soda or essential oils.

Ever since we'd launched the stick, I'd been at work developing this new formula. I planned to remove baking soda and adjust the ratios of the remaining ingredients, so formulating the recipe was almost like starting from scratch. And with the business requiring so much of my time and energy to be spent on CEO duties as it was, I wasn't exactly eager to spend my weekends formulating. But once I returned to the stove, spending dozens of Saturdays melting, mixing, and pouring, I became completely engrossed by the challenge. Often Oliver joined as my little assistant; I was glad when he found the process entertaining enough to stick around— I always wanted weekends to be about family time.

In the end, the winning replacement ingredient was magnesium, which I'd learned from previous research was a well-respected odor eliminator. The breakthrough came when I had the idea to use it in powder form, rather than milk of magnesia, which was sometimes used in liquid-based deodorant formulas. The powder form would complement the other ingredients in my formula, both in terms of texture and overall product performance. Incorporating it alongside my other prized ingredients was a breakthrough that resulted in a product unlike anything else on the market. The magnesium *really worked* and was effective for sensitive skin. After many iterations and adjustments, I finalized another formula that I was profoundly proud to have concocted myself in my little kitchen. And thanks to the extensive knowledge and experience I'd accumulated at this point, formulating it didn't take quite as long as developing the original stick version had. In addition to a fragrance-free option, I chose two other scents, Tea Tree and Geranium Flower, both of which smelled fresh and soothing, and were gentle on skin.

Chris and I talked extensively about a strategy for releasing the new sensitive skin line. Like the stick launch, this was big news for the company. Given how special the formula was, we saw an opportunity to distinguish them as a luxury offering. As such, we designed boxes to house individual units so they'd be positioned to compete with clinical strength formulas, which were commonly sold in boxes, too. It was a signal we were out to compete not just with other natural brands, but with conventional ones.

The team did careful research to determine a pricing structure. We considered affordability and accessibility, looking at what most customers were willing to spend per ounce and at their perception of value. While our current formulas were available for $8.99 on our website, we priced the sensitive skin options at $10.99, similar to existing clinical strength options. A recent natural deodorant upstart had begun to sell a "luxury" product that had an ingredient list similar to ours but with a $25 price tag on it—that wasn't what we were about.

For over a year, we'd kept a running log of every customer who had ever reported any skin sensitivity issue to us or asked about a sensitive skin formula. I hated when my customers were disappointed, and when we launched our sensitive skin deodorant, we immediately sent free products to those people who had reached out to us.

Expect not to know it *all*

With the launch of the sensitive skin line, we now needed to produce more deodorant than ever. Did we have enough staff? Enough supplies? I trusted Ben to oversee the back of house operations, but as we added more products and retailers—and ran accompanying marketing campaigns—the task was becoming exceedingly complex, and it was difficult to coordinate front and back of house operations. Occasionally, the marketing team would run a big buy-one-get-one promotion, and we would be slammed with more orders than our production and shipping teams could keep up with. We had strict turnaround times—any order placed through our website needed to be shipped within forty-eight hours—which became impossible to meet if we got hit with too many orders. On the opposite end of the spectrum, sometimes the volume of orders was lower than expected and we barely had enough shelving space to store all the finished product we had on hand. We were doing the best we could, but I knew we weren't operating as efficiently as possible.

There was some talk of working with a co-manufacturer, a manufacturer who we could hire to make the products for us, but we preferred producing in-house for the time being. I wanted to remain in close contact with my product. If there were any issues, I was literally on-site—just steps away—to consult with the team. I believed this was something our retailers and customers appreciated about us, too, especially given my story of starting in my kitchen. Plus, we found that most co-packers required very high order quantities, and while we were confidently growing, we didn't want to be locked into that. (I use the terms "co-packer," "co-manufacturer," and "contract manufacturer" interchangeably.)

Pros of working with outside parties

REAP THESE BENEFITS FROM WORKING WITH
CONSULTANTS AND AGENCIES

Innovation. Outside input can introduce you to new ways of thinking, helping to pull you out of a rut or fix a problem you don't yet realize you have.

Efficiency. Bringing in an agency, consultant, or proprietary technology can be cheaper and faster than onboarding employees. At Schmidt's, this was a huge benefit given the pace of growth we were experiencing.

Specialization. Specialists in a specific area of business (like manufacturing or AI that optimizes advertising campaigns) are able to offer niche insights that your employees can learn from and carry forward.

Shore up blind spots. Agencies are not meant to be a replacement for areas your company is already strong in. At Schmidt's, we partnered with an agency to support our manufacturing growth, and we worked with brokers, but thanks to Chris's marketing expertise, we were able to build out an in-house creative team that shot commercials for a fraction of the cost that agencies would have charged.

Through a connection, we learned about a local manufacturing consulting firm that might be able to provide help with our back of house operations. We brought them in, curious to see how we could improve. We had recently implemented a strategy of making as much product as possible so that we'd have plenty of deodorant on hand at any given time. Right away, the consultants pointed out the inefficiency in this approach: we were using up valuable floor space and restricting our cash flow by keeping so much money tied up in unsold product. They helped us rearrange the floorplan to optimize the flow of production and use of space. For example, as deodorant sticks came off the labeling line, they advised the team to begin packing them directly into boxes instead of adding an intermediate step by sitting them in a holding area first, then boxing them. Some of these small improvements seemed so obvious that I felt almost embarrassed for not having thought of them myself. But it wasn't like any of us had any experience running a manufacturing facility. It made me feel all the more grateful for the support.

The consultants also helped us operate with less inventory and with shorter manufacturing lead times, and instituted standard procedures around notifications, reporting, and communication. We tightened up our HR and hiring practices, and instituted more trainings. The consulting team proved so valuable that we kept them on board for much longer than initially planned, with a rep typically on-site two to three days a week. After about a year of working together, Schmidt's had increased our production capacity nearly tenfold and improved the efficiency of our staff by 50 percent. Best of all, our employees seemed genuinely happy to have more structure and to see the production process improved.

In July, I heard back from Target with incredible news: Schmidt's had been accepted, and they wanted to stock nearly two thousand stores across the country with Bergamot + Lime and Lavender + Sage. I practically jumped for joy out of my desk chair. Schmidt's was going to be in Target! When we told the team, we all shared an enthusiastic round of high-fives. Now, I thought, we'd *really* made it.

Turn make into manufacture

Getting prepared for this massive order was a huge, thrilling undertaking. The opening order was for over thirty thousand units of deodorant, which needed to get to Target by November in order to hit shelves in early February. In the meantime, we needed to scale up—again. We worked closely with our manufacturing consultants to evaluate the best way to prepare, and ultimately decided to bring in a second shift. I also established production leads and shift managers across all our teams, as well as individuals responsible for quality assurance. We hired a customer support manager and a few new customer support representatives, and upgraded our recently implemented software so that all customer communications could be carefully tracked. And it's a good thing we did, as it wasn't long before we were averaging upwards of ten thousand customer support tickets per month. Launching in Target, our first "mass market" store, meant reaching a much broader customer base—one that required more education and support, as many of these shoppers were new to natural products.

And remember that time I skimped and bought the recycled bar codes? It was time to buy new ones. In addition to Target, we were landing new retail accounts like Kroger, Walgreens, and CVS, and all required global standard barcodes. In the short term, that meant buying the barcodes and making label updates; in the long run, it meant a big headache for the company. Having two barcodes for the same product threw off our sales record-keeping and added a major layer of complication to our production process and inventory management.

When juggling it all started causing my head to spin, one strategy I implemented was asking employees to problem-solve and collaborate. If a manager had an issue to discuss with me, I'd ask her to prepare three possible solutions, along with the positives and negatives associated with each. That freed me up to devote more energy where I was really needed, and it was empowering for everyone. This made those "Jaime, we have a problem" moments less daunting.

In August, leaving behind Target preparations for a few days, I flew to Arkansas for a meeting with Walmart. Walking into their headquarters knowing we already had Target in our pocket was *huge*. I knew it would get their attention. Still, as I sat down across from the buyer, I could tell he was more of a stoic, no-nonsense businessman compared to other buyers. In some meetings, buyers expressed a genuine, personal enthusiasm for Schmidt's and for natural products, which always put me at ease and made for a more comfortable meeting. In this one, our conversation felt a lot more transactional, centering on how Schmidt's could meet a business need for their store. I worked hard to make a case for our value, and also became determined to connect with the buyer.

I'd googled him beforehand and learned that he was from Michigan, too. During the meeting, I kept waiting for the perfect moment to drop my Michigan bomb, though it never really presented itself. But, as our meeting wound to a close, I awkwardly blurted out something to the effect of "Yeah, when I was growing up in Michigan . . ." It caught his attention, and we casually chatted about our hometowns for a bit. Soon afterwards, we heard we had landed the account.

I was ecstatic. This was one of the largest companies in the *world*. Now, though, not only did we need to prepare to fulfill Target's order, but we had Walmart's on our docket, too. The opening order was relatively small, as a test run, but if all went well, we'd need to make and deliver hundreds of thousands more units (we hoped and expected) soon after the launch.

Before the real rush began, we launched a new scent: Rose + Vanilla. This was a special one for me, as the chosen scents had been crowdsourced from Schmidt's customers. How it happened: Chris and I had sent a newsletter and posted on social media asking customers to weigh in about which scent they wanted to see next. Thousands of responses came in. Ideas ranged from goofy to absurd to surprisingly delightful; people wanted deodorant that smelled like freshly cut grass, chocolate chip cookies, and mothballs reminiscent of Grandma's closet. We tallied all the feedback in a spreadsheet. By far, the two most popular suggestions were rose and vanilla. My challenge was to please my customers while also creating a scent that was interesting enough to be in line with the Schmidt's ethos. I stared at the spreadsheet and considered possibilities—maybe choosing vanilla or rose and trying it out with a suggestion further down on the list. Then I realized, they might actually work beautifully *together*. "Rose + Vanilla" looked and sounded really pleasing, and once combined, I surmised the scent would be special enough to fit in the Schmidt's family. I tested the combination. The result was sweet and elegant— I *loved* it. Plus, I recognized that the new scent would please a large subset of customers, both the ones who voted for vanilla and the ones who voted for rose.

Sure enough, when we launched Rose + Vanilla, we told customers it was thanks to them, and the scent was immediately well received, becoming our top seller. Compared to the early years, I had become pretty removed from my customers, and moments like this made me feel connected again. Hearing from them had always been so valuable for me, and even though that communication looked different now than it did during the farmers market days, it was just as important. My customers continued to be my focus group, my business plan, and my motivation.

Preparing for Target and Walmart was an all-hands-on-deck endeavor. Each team was hustling. Thankfully, Target's request for a dome-shaped stick and labels on the caps weren't actually all that complicated to put into place. In fact, these adjustments became our new way of manufacturing and were applied to all products to streamline for efficiency. I placed massive orders for raw materials, labels, and supplies. To cover the cost, the company took out a line of credit. We were going to need that cushion to see us through, especially because we anticipated a lag time of several months before we got paid.

The production team transitioned into two shifts, as planned. Because we needed to hire so many employees quickly, and for atypical work hours, we needed to work with staffing agencies to bring in temps. Our HR manager and I exhausted the resources of multiple staffing companies and eventually even held our own job fair, which resulted in some immediate hires. With *so* many new faces in the building—now over a hundred—sometimes I'd walk into the warehouse and I'd hardly be able to believe this was my company. The entire space was filled from wall to wall with multiple production lines, complete with ingredient prep stations, mixing areas, labeling tables, a cooling room, jar- and stick-filling stations, capping and finishing areas, as well as staging sections for packing and shipping, all abuzz with people working diligently while mixing and filling machines fired in the background at full bore. Our team was made up of people from all different cultural backgrounds, and it brought me so much satisfaction to watch as close friendships formed and employee-organized potlucks were held on a near-weekly basis. They were a happy, close-knit, dedicated group.

We were hiring so quickly that it was impossible for me to know everyone in the building. The break room was right across from my office, and sometimes when I heard a group of people chatting, I'd pop in to introduce myself. All it took was someone talking about their recipe for chile verde for me to jump up from my desk and say, "Are we sharing recipes?" Some were surprised to see a young woman CEO behind the business. Many of the temps knew little about the brand and were just there because their staffing company found them the job, though many did stay on and become full-time employees.

I also made an effort to have a presence on the production floor, stopping to check in with people and show interest in what they were doing. It was amazing to see how the production process had morphed since my initial days of making. I always felt closer to the product and the team afterwards, and the time spent back of house provided a much-needed break from the nonstop emails and problem-solving that consumed my days. The marketing cubicles were just down the hallway from my office, and I often spent time with that team, too, jumping in to hear about what they were working on and offering input. I became notorious for "popping in," which showed employees I cared, and made me feel more connected to everyone. Chris and I also began holding quarterly stand-up meetings to share updates about new product launches and retail placements, plus in-office celebrations for holidays and special events. Seeing a hundred plus employees in *my* factory, working for *me*, was surreal.

With more people producing more deodorant, bumps in the road were inevitable. On one occasion, a batch of thousands of units was mislabeled by the second shift. We needed to unpack the products, strip off the incorrect labels, and reapply new ones. Our manufacturing consultants had helped us put safeguards against errors in place, like keeping labels with the different bar codes locked in separate storage areas, and implementing a procedure where the person changing the labels signs off on a form to confirm the task was completed properly. However, mistakes still happened, and this was a costly one.

Despite the inevitable stumbles of scaling so quickly, by November we had managed to complete our opening orders for Target and Walmart and get them out the door. There was no time to slow down, though. With the holidays around the corner, we launched our first limited-edition scent, Spruce + Spice, and promoted it heavily. Customers couldn't wait to try it. By the end of 2016, we had earned $6.9 million in revenue—a stunning 350 percent increase over the year before. The pace of growth was relentless and often stressful, and while I was often on the verge of burnout, each new accomplishment provided fresh motivation to keep going. At the office, we intentionally created a culture of celebration. Whenever we won an award or earned a big headline or account, the whole team celebrated. The collective enthusiasm continually energized us. And then I'd quickly set my sights on the next win. ■

What to make of it

 Decide where to keep your hands dirty.

Learning to delegate is difficult but crucial. As our team expanded rapidly, I had to put trust in our consultants and department heads so that I could focus on what I needed to do to keep the business thriving. In fact, letting go enabled me to be a better leader.

 Foster internal communication.

As Schmidt's grew, I wanted to make sure everyone felt connected to the mission and to each other. We developed an internal "magazine" with updates and employee quotes and features. I sent regular staff-wide emails in which I'd call out teams' accomplishments. We made a book of press features and put it in the break room so employees could see how well the products they made were being received. And we put up a bulletin board where employees could pin positive comments about one another.

 Customers should continue to be your focus group, your business plan, and your motivation.

Not only was healthy internal communication critical, but so was maintaining a strong connection with customers. I loved that I could still tap into direct feedback and turn it into a business decision for Schmidt's, like when we developed Rose + Vanilla. Continually finding ways to talk with my customers led to success—and personal fulfillment—time and again.

Part IV

Make It

Last

Sustain your product
+ stay true to your path

CHAPTER 10

Broaden your vision.

When I'm asked about what made Schmidt's so successful, I often say that my customers were my business plan. It started when I listened to those at the farmers market, and it continued through each step of growth. Staying hyper-tuned in to my customers always guided and served me.

As our customer base grew, requests for other products grew louder. Customers wanted to smell like Schmidt's from head to toe. (Personally, I did, too.) Adding soaps in the same scents as our original deodorant line seemed an obvious and fun next step.

Toothpaste was another product customers constantly asked about, and it was a category we knew was ready for something new. We started to think about how Schmidt's could expand into the rest of the bathroom routine, establishing us as a full personal care brand. With the strong fan base we'd established, the opportunities felt limitless.

Back in 2012, when I chose to eliminate my other products to make and sell only deodorant, the decision marked my first big strategic business move—one that solidified my commitment to being *the* natural deodorant maker in Portland.

In 2017, five years later, to say everything had changed would be an understatement. Schmidt's had grown beyond my wildest imagination. I had gone from being a one-woman show to leading a 150-employee company with no slowdown in sight. I was increasingly pulled toward executive duties while still playing a big role in developing new products, like our soon-to-be released Charcoal + Magnesium scent. So much had changed, and I had, too. I was ready to grow beyond deodorant.

At the outset of 2017, we began doing business as Schmidt's Naturals and announced an expanded vision for the company. We launched an updated website and refreshed our brand identity, removing the red "natural deodorant" from the Schmidt's logo, brightening and tightening up our color palette, updating our fonts to more modern typefaces, and incorporating new botanical illustrations in our designs. A big year lay ahead—much bigger than I even knew at the time.

Break through to the mainstream

Fulfilling our opening orders for Target and Walmart was just the first step in maintaining these massive new accounts. We needed to make sure the launch was a huge success, and we needed to shift our attention toward investing in the infrastructure of our company in order to maintain our sales momentum. It was one thing to get on shelves at these big retailers, and another altogether to actually move enough units to stay competitive.

First, we had to deliver on promises made to each store to make our launch go off without a hitch. When we pitched

Target, we found out how many units a competing natural deodorant sold per product, per week, and used our sales data from other retailers to convince them we could sell 50 percent more. We also shared case studies demonstrating that Schmidt's wouldn't just be a swap for other brands. Instead of cannibalizing sales, we showed how Schmidt's would bring new, trend-savvy customers into stores who would spend more during a store visit and trade up from their old deodorant. We also committed to $100,000 in promotions, which meant we'd discount our products and participate in other promotional partnerships. Anytime Target offered our customers a discount, say 10 percent off, Schmidt's would pay Target that 10 percent so the store still made the full amount. Budgeting for promotions showed Target we were committed to making Schmidt's fly off the shelves. At launch, we planned to go with a big 20-percent-off push and follow up shortly thereafter with a buy-one-get-one sale.

Show your commitment to retailers

TECHNIQUES TO LAND DEALS AND BUILD STRONG RETAILER RELATIONSHIPS

Promo. Saying yes to promotion opportunities shows retailers you're committed to your partnership. Promos at launch are particularly important to show strong sales numbers right out of the gate.

Store-specific ads. Help drive traffic into stores by advertising to your audience that your products are now available at a specific retailer. Remember, retailers want to see that your brand is driving *new* traffic into their stores rather than sabotaging sales of a brand they already have on their shelves.

In-store demos and staff trainings. Send team members to train on-site staff about your product so they're empowered to talk about it with customers, and/or show up for in-store demos to connect with customers directly.

Giveaways. Retailers will often ask you to supply products for in-store events and giveaways. Say yes to show your support.

Chris and the marketing team were hard at work preparing for the Target launch. They created dozens of campaigns rolling out store-specific ads for Facebook and Google, targeting people within ten miles of a store. Facebook ads, for example, included a map with a Schmidt's destination pin and messaging about how we were now available in Target.

In his role as marketing executive, Chris made the decision to expand his department into three teams: Digital Marketing (advertising, analyzing campaign performance, overseeing digital assets), Brand (establishing our voice and mission, managing communications, PR, and social media), and Creative. Of all these, I stayed most hands-on with the Brand team, making sure our voice and vision remained authentic and relevant—I saw this as one of the most crucial ways we stood out from the competition. Nearly every piece of Schmidt's content showed real people in real settings; the models for our photo shoots were intentionally chosen to look like the vibrant, diverse people who made up our customer base. And, we responded to cultural happenings in the moment (like when dyeing your armpit hair à la Miley Cyrus became a thing, or when Whole Foods was acquired by Amazon).

When it came to copy, everything sounded like it was coming from a real person with our specific brand voice (smart, conversational, confident). We never used lingo like "Check us out" or "What are you waiting for?" Calls to action were more likely to be "Which scent will you choose?" than "Give our Rose + Vanilla deodorant a try!" Anytime we responded to a comment online, the goal was to be friendly and conversational, inviting the customer to keep talking. If someone left a comment about loving a scent, instead of replying with a heart-eyes emoji or a "Thanks!" we'd say something like, "Yes! I wore Cedarwood + Juniper today on a hike. Do you switch up your scent depending on your plans for the day?" We encouraged customers to talk to each other online, too. Instead of stepping in immediately in all conversations, we'd stand by to see if one commenter might offer a tip or suggestion to another, thereby fostering a sense of community. And when we did need to chime in to address a question or concern, we strove to be as proactive and helpful as possible. If someone said their skin was irritated, we had a blog post we could point them to explaining best practices for application, the benefits of our sensitive skin line, or our customer support and exchange policy. We kept a close eye on search results associated with Schmidt's and other deodorant brands, and developed blog content around the most common issues we saw (stained clothing, excessive sweating, concerns about aluminum). This drove huge amounts of traffic, keeping us at the top of organic search results.

Instagram analytics tools helped us identify top commenters and followers, along with influencers, who we would then build relationships with. We commented on their posts (even if they had nothing to do with deodorant), sent DMs, and had real conversations. There were no shortcuts to building our audience; to earn organic engagement, we made real connections. We even developed an exclusive program for our top supporters called the Rose Society, extending offers for free products and early access to our newest releases. When we did do paid sponsorships, we worked with "micro-influencers" (people considered experts in a niche, with somewhere between a thousand and ten thousand followers), which felt like a more natural fit for our brand and audience.

Whereas early digital marketing strategies focused entirely on being profitable and expanding our customer base, the success of those campaigns allowed the team to expand into awareness-building efforts. Now, a portion of our advertising budget went toward ensuring people across the country had heard of Schmidt's or had a positive perception of us—thereby increasing their likelihood of becoming a customer. Especially exciting to me was a series of commercials Chris and I were developing with our Director of Creative, which would air across television networks, Hulu, YouTube, and on social media. With a huge influx in the amount of business now generated by retail, awareness would become even more important. Conventional brands were now our direct competition, not just those in the natural category.

We needed customers to have at least had an inkling of who we were. For many who had seen Schmidt's online but never purchased it, picking us up at Walmart or Target was their first opportunity to switch.

In January 2017, shortly before the Target and Walmart launch, we debuted our subscription builder (allowing shoppers on our website to sign up for a Schmidt's delivery of their choosing monthly, or every two, three, or four months) and focused more on the lifetime value of a customer (how much they would spend over time, rather than just in the moment). So even if we spent more money acquiring customers than usual, we trusted that if a customer on average would purchase 2.5 times (and hopefully turn on some friends in the process), that money would come back to us down the line.

So by the time we launched in Target and Walmart, we'd built up a thriving audience of Schmidt's enthusiasts who respected our brand or had at least heard of it. When Schmidt's hit shelves in Target, we saw immediate success and Target's sales numbers showed we were quickly outselling conventional brands on a per unit basis. Target hadn't expected the huge volume of instant sales, and it took their automated reordering system some time to catch up with the demand. Stores were regularly out of stock. That same month, when we launched in Walmart, we saw similar success.

I would often find excuses to stop by these stores just to see my product on the shelves and even sometimes snap a photo. The excitement was real! And when I'd run into an acquaintance, I was often greeted with, "I saw your product at Target the other day!" Or a friend might tell me their kids were excited to run to the deodorant aisle in stores to spot

Schmidt's. It was a turning point for me and the way I saw the business (and myself). Schmidt's had truly become a household name—something I'd dreamt about from almost the very beginning.

Chris, Michael, and I went out to celebrate the successful launch and all that was to come with drinks at a local lounge. This kicked off a series of celebrations among the three of us, where we would leave work together to strategize over cocktails. We frequently all got lunch together at a hidden gem Thai spot near the office. I was determined to maintain our partnership and would try to prioritize these kinds of casual hangouts. Aside from some inconsistencies, the three of us worked well together, and it seemed each of us filled in the gaps where another might have been lacking.

Share what you shoulder

Despite the celebrations and success, most of the time I remained so deep in work mode that it was hard to take it all in. Everything was happening at once; even when an amazing development took place, I had to keep my attention on our team and on next steps in order to keep up. From finance, to legal, to operations, to sales, to press interviews (and everything else), my attention was in constant demand.

Recently I had brought on Gabriella, a strategic and highly experienced hire who was now the Operations Manager, in charge of everything back of house (I was happy to have Ben working alongside her, remaining an integral part of our team). But I still had my hands in just about everything. Even though there were people taking the lead in every department, employees still came to me with problems, and there was always a fire to put out. After we shipped out our opening orders for Target and Walmart, we released the temps we'd brought on, since their job was done (or so we thought) and we didn't want to overproduce. Soon after, though, we discovered several huge overlooked orders from other retailers buried on an arrowroot powder–covered desk. Now we had a serious backlog and had to rehire the workers we'd just dismissed. Embarrassing, and a waste of time!

Then there was a shipping bottleneck, as we were producing faster than we were able to pack and ship. In order to keep up, we needed to hire more staff specifically for shipping. But space was incredibly tight; we were simply running out of room in the warehouse to fit additional employees. Again.

Around this time, we purchased a second filling machine to keep up with demand—but we had no place to plug it in. These machines required a special electrical hookup that we didn't have. We discussed various options before making an urgent call to the electrician to remedy the situation.

At one point, we'd been waiting on a big delivery of shea butter when we heard the truck carrying our shipment had been in an accident and had tipped over on the highway. An email arrived in my inbox with the subject "Order delay." Inside was a photo of the highway strewn with boxes of shea butter.

The demands of maintaining an efficiently operated, scalable production facility were enormous, and it felt like there was a new one every day. What had begun as *making* was now *manufacturing*. The continuous multitasking drained me and made me feel less effective; instead of focusing on one thing and doing it well, I was continuously trying to juggle it all.

Our teams and consultants, despite their positive attitudes, were being pushed to the max. Schmidt's had grown to the point where it made sense to hire industry veterans for executive leadership positions, like a COO and VP of Sales, and that option was certainly on my radar. In order to sustain the company's expansion, we needed help.

In February, around the same time that we launched in Target and Walmart, we also met with an investment bank to explore getting connected with interested investors. Schmidt's had been self-funded and profitable since the beginning, but we were reaching the limit of what we could accomplish independently. To sustain the growth ahead—including getting to the next level, Costco (COSTCO!)—we'd need financial support. The upfront cash it would require to fulfill an opening order from Costco alone would be tremendous. No fast-growing business like ours has that kind of money just sitting around, so, naturally, we couldn't fund the four hundred thousand deodorant sticks (490 pallets, each with 270 packs, three sticks per pack!). We began exploring other options for funding and paid closer attention to the incoming letters of interest from investment firms.

Shortly after Gabriella joined the team at the end of 2016, we made plans to scale Schmidt's production with a contract manufacturer. The deodorant was my creation, and I'd been personally responsible for overseeing and managing it from the beginning. But it was time to share that responsibility. We'd successfully produced those opening orders for Target and Walmart, but we needed support to keep up with demand. Our goal was to have the contract manufacturer fulfill the large orders for those accounts (along with a few others), while the Portland production team managed the rest. This would enable us to meet demand, as well as continue innovating and releasing limited-edition products via our Portland facility. Having a co-manufacturer also meant we'd have a backup in the event of a disaster. What if something tragic were to occur, like a natural disaster impacting the warehouse? We couldn't afford not to have a safety net.

Gabriella and I flew across the country to our new co-manufacturing partner early in 2017. The company was the most reputable and established deodorant co-manufacturer in the world, working with all the big names in deodorant, and we felt comfortable knowing they'd be able to handle the quantities we now required. When we arrived, the magnitude and sophistication of their capabilities was both humbling and reassuring. They'd never worked with a formula quite like ours; most other deodorants are made with a high volume of water and other filler ingredients—much different from the dense concoction of butters and powders in Schmidt's. We worked long days together to perfect the process, cutting deodorant sticks in half and examining the product closely, and refining techniques in the manufacturing process until it was perfect. The co-manufacturer's quality control capabilities were advanced, with benchmarks across a multitude of product properties, from color to density, to precise weights, volumes, and hold times. We took back some of these standards and implemented them in our own warehouse.

Collaboration considerations
WHAT TO EVALUATE WHEN TAKING ON A CO-PACKER OR
CONTRACT MANUFACTURER

Quality controls. What type of quality control processes are in place? How do they ensure that standards are being met and that there's consistency across batches? Most established co-packers should easily be able to share their criteria.

Capacity capabilities. What capacities can the co-packer handle? They may seem a good fit when demand is lower, but as you scale, will they be able to keep up? Conversely, the co-packer may have minimum order requirements, which you'll want to ensure don't create a surplus.

Process. What is the system for ordering and handling raw materials? You need to consider how much of this you prefer to control and what you want to hand over. Keep in mind, having them take over ordering ingredients, etc., means you will be revealing your suppliers, and it's sometimes wise to keep this information proprietary.

Confidentiality. What kind of controls will you have over your formulas and recipes? The last thing you want is for a new competitor to partner up with the same co-packer who reuses your recipe. Keep in mind that many of these things are negotiable and can be worked into your agreements. A nondisclosure agreement is a must regardless of the scope of the agreement.

Location. The further away the co-packer is from your office, the harder it will be to drop in for visits. Shipping costs of finished product and raw materials are something to consider, too.

While I had felt anxious about losing control over some of the production process, the feeling I had when I boarded the plane back to Portland was much closer to relief. I knew my deodorant was in good hands. Still, since I'd become quite guarded about the recipes I'd worked so hard to perfect, we implemented a system where we premixed all powders and oils at our facility before shipping them to the contract manufacturer. That way, they wouldn't have access to my precise formula. We partnered with a distribution center close to the new co-manufacturer so that the finished product could be shipped to some of our accounts more efficiently, and within a few months, they were up and running.

Just because our company was scaling so significantly with our existing products didn't mean I stopped creating new ones. In March, Schmidt's launched Charcoal + Magnesium, which became an instant top seller, followed by two more sensitive skin scents: Jasmine Tea and Coconut Pineapple. These three were fun to develop, not only because scent exploration always ignited my passion for making, but also because it gave me a refreshing break from the operational side of the business.

For scents that aren't available as essential oils (like pineapple), specialized fragrance houses can mimic the smell using natural fruit/plant extracts called isolates. You can get pretty close to a pineapple scent, it turns out, with isolates of tree sap and certain flowers. I worked with one of our fragrance houses to perfect Jasmine Tea, inspired by one of my and Chris's favorite teas, and Coconut Pineapple, a bright, tropical option I felt had been missing from our lineup. Charcoal + Magnesium was one of our most sophisticated and adventurous scents, reminiscent of freshly fallen rain on concrete (in the fragrance world, we call this petrichor or ozone) with top notes of fresh citrus.

We always worked with at least two fragrance houses at a time to make sure we were getting the most spot-on scents, highest quality products, and competitive prices (and of course as backup to ensure we never ran out of supply). I'd developed close relationships at the fragrance houses and would tell them which scents I was interested in exploring, and they'd send a variety of samples. It was always exciting when a delivery of new scents showed up on my desk. I'd quickly stop whatever I was doing (regardless of how urgent), and eagerly tear into the box filled with little amber bottles. There was often a quick *ewww, no*, some *hmm, maybes*, and occasionally an *ooh, that's nice*. The *ooh, that's nice* ones would earn a place at my desk for further consideration. I built up quite the collection over the years and would sometimes dig into my own stash for additional inspiration and tweaks.

Before we introduced our Charcoal + Magnesium deodorant, we saw in industry reports that charcoal was a trending ingredient in personal care products, with large volumes of Google search interest. Additionally, another deodorant brand had launched its own version of a charcoal deodorant, which was performing successfully. After analyzing these reports, we started considering how we might formulate our own. It was becoming clear that more customers were interested in charcoal, and we wanted to provide a spin on a version that would compete with—and outperform (always our goal!)—the rest. We wanted to be unique (hence Charcoal + *Magnesium*, with a distinct label and scent direction), but participating in a trend is oftentimes a smart business move. Developing the formula required more kitchen time for me, this time to perfect the ratio of charcoal, magnesium, arrowroot powder, and baking soda. When I nailed the combination, I referred to it as my new "hybrid" formula, as it had ingredients from both my original and sensitive skin versions, plus the addition of charcoal. It was everything I loved about both formulas combined into one (perfect texture and efficacy), and I was proud to again be innovating with a new use of ingredients in deodorant.

Soon after those launches, Chris walked into my office one day and said, "We need a limited-edition summer scent." Summer was just weeks away, but I loved the idea and knew one of the oils I'd saved in my desk drawer would offer the perfect beachy, tropical scent. Chris thought up the name: Waves. The same day, he alerted the design team, who immediately started creating the label artwork in partnership with a local illustrator, with a fun new "wavy" font that was illustrated by hand. We made two versions, one in my new hybrid formula (minus the charcoal) and one in the sensitive skin version, and prepared to launch as soon as we could. Later, I came to understand that it's a wise business precaution to stability-test any new scent before launch, which is a process that takes several months. Eventually this became a non-negotiable part of our research phase, but at the time, Schmidt's was still small enough to move quickly, and I trusted my formulas to remain stable from scent to scent, which they always did.

As we prepared to launch, we formed a partnership with the Surfrider Foundation, donating 5 percent of Waves proceeds to the organization in support of its work to combat ocean pollution. We also participated in a big beach cleanup event in tandem with our launch. A collaboration like this was good for publicity, but, more importantly, now that we had the budget, I really wanted to give back in a way that was in keeping with the company's and my customers' values. Our employees were excited to contribute to a good cause, too, and it was fun and meaningful to rally behind something together.

Once your track record is proven, do more

That was the fun part. But we had a much bigger task at hand: the new products we'd been thinking about. Though we had been talking about it for some time, there was never an ideal moment to focus on the task, given the ever-changing, ever-growing nature of the business. In 2017, I made new products a priority, starting with soap and toothpaste. I, of course, led on formulating, while Chris took the lead on research, as he knew our audience better than anyone and was familiar with trend reports and consumer insight data.

The days of stirring up concoctions in my kitchen were over. When it came to formulating soap and toothpaste, we collaborated with co-packers to nail down the formulas. I met many at expos, and several sent us samples of soaps and toothpastes they were already manufacturing. Chris and I examined countless varieties, making our own judgments on which textures, colors, and shapes we preferred. Oliver had his own opinions, which he tracked in a little Schmidt's notebook with "product development" written across the front in his sweet seven-year-old handwriting. We submitted lists of ingredients we wanted to use (like unique exfoliants for soap), as well as ones we didn't (synthetic dyes or the foaming agent SLS—sodium laureth sulfate).

Working on soap was fun for me. It was liberating to explore lather, bar shapes, and exfoliants without the same kind of pressure I'd felt in the performance territory of deodorant. I maintained my own incredibly high standards for the scent—they needed to smell just like the deodorant fragrances I'd developed, accomplished by using the same oils. There were new considerations about texture: how they felt in my hands, how they lathered, and the way they made my skin feel.

I intentionally sought out a range of unique exfoliants, from bamboo to volcanic sand to jojoba seeds, careful to make sure each one had the right amount of texture and wasn't too abrasive. Once again, customer preference guided my decision-making: from consumer surveys, I knew that exfoliating agents were especially important to people, so I invested time and research into which ones seemed to harmonize well with our other products. In the end, I paired Bergamot + Lime with exfoliating orange peel; Rose + Vanilla with vanilla bean; Lavender + Sage with jojoba seed; Ylang-Ylang + Calendula with apricot seed; and Cedarwood + Juniper with volcanic sand. Color mattered, too. For my favorite scent, Ylang-Ylang + Calendula, we added turmeric to achieve a beautiful golden yellow and chlorophyll to nail a soft, sea green hue for Bergamot + Lime. I chose a smooth, sturdy size and shape that felt natural in my hands. The Schmidt's logo was debossed across the top (so cool), which I requested be deep enough to last through many showers. The same design team I'd worked with on my original rebrand created the boxes, which matched the colors and illustrations perfected for our deodorant.

While soap is a natural extension of deodorant, toothpaste was a whole new creative adventure. I ordered dozens of existing brands, and Chris and I tried them all out at home, taking notes on the whole sensory experience. We spent the better part of a night side by side in front of the bathroom sink, commenting through mouthfuls of foam about what we thought of a certain flavor, texture, or mouthfeel, laughing at ourselves as our mouths went numb from all the mint. We mailed our favorites to our co-packer with notes about what we liked, then waited for custom samples they'd create based on our feedback. We also provided a list of claims we wanted to be able to make about our product, for example, that it be free of SLS, polyethylene glycol (PEG), phthalates, artificial sweeteners, and dyes. I was motivated to put out the cleanest, healthiest formulas, so it was incredibly important for me to avoid those kinds of ingredients. But I also wanted to include innovative ones, unlike traditional formulas on the shelves. So many natural toothpastes focused on what *wasn't* in the product. I wanted Schmidt's to get customers excited about what *was* in the product. We put together the perfect pairing of ingredients with added benefits: vitamins, superfood extracts like goji and pomegranate, magnolia bark extract, organic aloe leaf juice, charcoal, and more. Later we even decided to call it a "tooth + mouth" paste, as the formula went beyond cleaning teeth and was designed to support whole mouth health.

Both soap and toothpaste remained in the works throughout the better half of 2017 as we iterated toward a place where I could be proud of them and confident about adding them to Schmidt's offerings. We also started building a product roadmap with everything we wanted to eventually see with the Schmidt's name on it, even beyond personal care products. (Fast-forward to the fall of 2019, when the brand expanded into cleaning products with our new lines of laundry detergents and cleaning sprays!) In July, I hired Alyssa, the first member of my new product development team. She relocated from Ohio where she had been a senior innovator at one of the consumer packaged goods (CPG) giants. I was excited to pick her brain and have her on the team—someone with proven expertise and a different perspective coming from the more corporate scene.

Moving beyond your signature product

QUESTIONS TO ASK WHEN CONSIDERING EXPANDING YOUR PRODUCT LINE

Fit. Does the product complement your existing offerings and make sense for your brand story?

Desirability. Do your customers want it? Use surveys and analytics to understand the desires of your existing customer base.

Competition. Are you fully aware of the competitive landscape and what you're up against? In the earlier days, launching a new product can be less risky, but for a more established brand, a failed product launch can cause a major setback.

Retail viability. Are your retailers interested in making shelf space for a product like this from your brand? Talk to them about it.

Production. Can you utilize your existing technologies and manufacturing capabilities to produce it (including relationships with contract manufacturers), or will you need a big capital investment to start from scratch?

Preserve your brand's legacy

In 2017, there was an electrifying buzz in the air about Schmidt's. It was the new normal for press features and awards to arrive one after another. At the start of the year, we began working with a second PR firm to help us tell the story of how Schmidt's came to be. Most of our media coverage up to that point had been focused on the deodorant itself, or standard Q&As with me, but I believed that telling my founding story served as a point of differentiation for us, especially as the brand continued to grow. One of our biggest opportunities to do so came from *Forbes*. Titled "How Schmidt's Naturals Made Deodorant in a Jar Fashionable," the feature was one of the first ones to highlight the origins and people behind the brand. When it went live online, I eagerly began reading on my computer at work. But as I scanned the opening lines, I felt a pit form in the bottom of my stomach (and not just because they spelled my name wrong).

"When entrepreneur Michael Cammarata was considering investing in Jamie Schmidt's natural deodorant," the opening line read, "he was skeptical, after all, the product was in jars with a popsicle stick as an applicator, but he only had to look at her customer base to understand he had found something unique."

The article continued with background on how the company had started as a hobby of mine when I was pregnant, then read, "When Cammarata found Schmidt in 2014, she was still working out of her home in Portland, OR . . . Very quickly after getting involved Cammarata and Schmidt outgrew her home kitchen and went to a five thousand-square-foot facility within three months, and then outgrew that and went to a fourteen thousand-square-foot facility six months later."

Aside from basic inaccuracies (like spelling my name wrong, and the fact that I was *not* working out of my kitchen when I met Michael and Kevin), the article painted me as a hobbyist who had been "found." Weird.

I messaged Chris, who was just as confused as I was. We got our PR firm on the phone, who were relatively dismissive of my concerns, saying how writers sometimes perceive things differently and write up their own version. I moved on with a note to self that I would need to be more intentional about making sure my story was protected and told factually, from my role in founding and growing the company to the titles I had held.

I never cared much about titles, and, frankly, I sometimes see them as a little ego-driven. But, I'd operated as Schmidt's CEO for years throughout our growth, signing my title on endless emails, contracts, and more. For many startup entrepreneurs, being thrust into an executive role just comes with the territory, and I chose to embrace those three initials with pride, whether my products were selling in thirty stores or thirty thousand.

My advice is to protect your history by keeping detailed records and backups of all your files and correspondences. That way, there can be no disputing the facts later, should any nuisance arise.

Around the same time, I was approached by Ernst & Young, who invited me to apply for their Entrepreneur of the Year award: "Dear Press Team, I wanted to reach out and share information on a unique program EY produces, EY Entrepreneur of the Year® as I believe Jaime Schmidt would make a great candidate. Now in its 31st year, Entrepreneur of the Year remains one of the top competitive awards in the world for entrepreneurs and leaders of high-growth companies." When Michael heard the news of my being solicited, he felt strongly that we should apply as a pair, and in the spirit of teamwork I agreed. We underwent a lengthy process to participate that included multiple interviews in Seattle and Portland, and we were selected as finalists! The winners would be announced at a fancy gala in Seattle in front of five hundred influential attendees. Chris was convinced we were going to win and made it a special event, recruiting many from the Schmidt's team to join us and make the drive in a party limousine. As dinner ended and the ceremony began, I ran off to the bathroom to freshen up my hair and makeup, without realizing that our category was first. When I walked back into the ballroom, there was my face on the big screen. Winning the award was one of the most gratifying moments of my career, and it felt like the first time I'd been recognized for my work in a professional setting. As I walked toward the stage, I took the little piece of paper on which I'd written speaking points and threw it under the stage, choosing instead to wing it at the mic. I thanked everyone I could think of, smiling so much my cheeks hurt. Afterwards the whole team celebrated late into the night.

It was a big moment! However, another issue about our company story—similar to what happened with the *Forbes* article—had come up in the Ernst & Young selection process. In advance of the big event, Ernst & Young requested each finalist be interviewed by a production team for a short video. Our new PR team drafted and emailed speaking points for Michael and me in advance, but I was put off by what they provided.

Similar to the *Forbes* feature, the talking points described some Cinderella story about how Michael had "found" me, at which time my business was propelled into success. This is a reflection of a deeper issue in today's culture where the contributions of women leaders are positioned as secondary to men's. It's a problem all around the world, and it has long been time for this to change.

Listen to the market (and your intuition)

Throughout the spring of 2017, we worked with our investment bank to schedule calls and meetings with a variety of hedge funds, private equity firms, and venture capital groups. We'd been entertaining giving up anywhere from 5 to 30 percent equity in exchange for funding for the next two to three years. But by mid-2017, things were shifting.

Several big-name funds had entered the picture, and a few wanted to acquire the company outright.

Then came some of the largest players in the CPG industry—I was floored when they too showed interest in acquiring us. This was the real deal. The big names in personal care seemed to be catching on that natural deodorant was the way of the future. All the major players were at the table, and it gave us a lot of room to negotiate for a higher valuation.

By now—thanks primarily to countless pitch meetings with retail accounts—we were quite practiced at pitching, reading the room, and fielding tough questions. I opened dozens of presentations by sharing my story of founding Schmidt's and examples of our success, then Chris would dive deep into our brand proposition and data. He'd developed a thorough presentation of everything we had accomplished together over the years, and he delivered it with conviction. Michael was often quiet in these meetings, but behind the scenes he was great at establishing personal relationships with lead people on the other side.

The natural personal care products industry had blown up, and it was becoming clear that these large CPG companies were eager to find a way in. We'd heard from our contacts at Target and Walmart that their stores were going to be building out significant natural products shelves—room for more brands than they'd ever allotted space for before. The movement toward natural was real, and Schmidt's was at the forefront.

I knew we needed cash to sustain the business, but selling it outright had never been part of my thinking. Once serious interest came in from these big, reputable, long-standing companies, I started to realize a part of me—a big part— would feel relieved to place my business under their guidance and expertise. Schmidt's was becoming a household name. It was an amazing feat—one I was incredibly proud of—but it also left me feeling exposed. What if we were to suddenly go bankrupt due to some kind of unpredictable disaster or mishap? We could get pulled from Target's shelves permanently; the business could go under. While I trusted the team I'd built, anxious thoughts like these kept me up at night. How long could I sustain this massive growth? Adding to this, my stress level was at its max, and my health had moved down in my list of priorities.

We'd finally landed our nationwide placement with Whole Foods, and in July, when we had our big meeting with Costco, I left the meeting knowing in my gut we had landed the deal. Soon after, we got the confirmation. I was really excited, but I also knew what this meant: another huge growth spurt, when we were still adjusting to the demands of selling in Target and Walmart. We needed cash, we needed expertise, we needed to hire. It felt like an increasingly heavy burden to navigate through the treacherous waters of global expansion and competition.

As much as I felt I was living the dream with running my own business, I couldn't help but entertain thoughts about what life could be like for Chris, Oliver, and me if we were less tied to the risks and obligations of the company I'd built. In the previous few years, any travel I did was strictly for business, and I had essentially no time for casual hangouts with friends. My life was motherhood and Schmidt's. I'd catch myself imagining how things might be easier or more compartmentalized with a less strenuous job. I pictured home-cooked dinners, bike rides after school with Oliver, vacations with my family back in Michigan, time for exercise, and evenings out with Chris where deodorant wasn't mentioned even once.

Once the opportunity to sell the company was on the table and we had time to discuss it and warm up to it, Chris and I agreed that it seemed like the right move. Like me, there were times he felt confined by what we'd built. "Think about all we could do to help others, and the kind of life we could live, without all this pressure," we would say. ■

What to make of it

 Your brand drives attention to your product.

Having an excellent product was our foundation, but it was our brand personality that took customers from "I need natural deodorant" to "I need Schmidt's." Honing our brand's identity was a continual, evolving effort. Never let your brand go static. Be consistent in keeping it real (on brand) but continue to push it forward.

 Know when to expand your vision.

Customers wanted more from Schmidt's than deodorant. Listening to them helped us understand when the timing was right to expand. But it required over a year of research to determine what direction we would take with soap and toothpaste, and to develop them in a way that was in keeping with Schmidt's values. Be open to expanding your vision, but don't rush in.

 Understand the market.

We were getting signs that the natural products space was heating up to a critical point, and that selling the company might be on the table for only a specific window of time. And with multiple giant companies showing interest, we had to recognize the negotiating power that afforded us. We couldn't just walk away, then expect them to all be interested again in a few years. If it was going to happen, it was going to happen now. Once again, I found I had to move quickly.

CHAPTER 11

Power through.

E ven though I viewed an acquisition as the best way to secure the company's future, and that of my family, the idea of relinquishing control of Schmidt's was difficult to wrap my mind around. Schmidt's was my passion and my product. Many of my colleagues were like family. In seven years running the company, I'd learned so much and had grown in so many ways. I had an intimate, hands-on connection with my products and with nearly every other aspect of the business that had followed. What would it mean to pass all that on to someone else? Could I really be sure Schmidt's values would remain intact? That my vision would be carried forward? There was so much potential in selling the company, but I resolved to do it only if I knew Schmidt's would be in the best hands.

While Chris and I had become increasingly excited by the prospect of selling the company, we also knew we couldn't count on it happening. Anything could go awry; any potential deal could fall through. By now Schmidt's had grown to 150 employees, each of whom was relying on us for stability and a salary. We were on pace to more than triple 2016's revenue, with nearly $23 million for the year. We continued running and growing the company, knowing there was no guarantee an acquisition would happen.

Guide your employees and customers through growth

In July, we opened a satellite office in Orlando, where we would house some of our customer support and sales employees. Several months prior, we had also outsourced a finance firm out of Sarasota to help with budgeting and fore-casting. This meant a substantial part of the Schmidt's team was on the other side of the country.

In Portland, we acquired another six thousand square feet when our neighbors moved out, bringing us to fifteen thousand square feet. But we quickly maxed out the entire space and began talks about finding a new space for the fourth time in three years. The bigger we grew, the harder it became to move. Even though we devoted the entirety of the new space to shipping, it still wasn't enough; we were bursting at the seams. Instead of breaking the lease and uprooting everything by looking for an even bigger warehouse, we decided it made the most sense to split up the teams, with the marketing and product development teams moving to their own office so the back, of the house teams could take over the entire warehouse. The Portland customer support team stayed back, too, to be close to shipping and production for ease of communication. Ben, Darcy, Gabriella, and team leads now had room to spread out, not to mention powder-free areas in which to do their paperwork. We spent months searching for an office space in downtown Portland and finally, in August 2017, we moved into the space previously occupied by Under

Armour. I liked the idea of inheriting some of the brand's successful energy in the new space.

One of the noticeable differences of the new office was just how quiet it was. We were so used to the sounds of machines running all day (including a particularly cacophonous air compressor for stick filling) that, by contrast, the new office felt serene. Three stories up, we kept the windows open, letting the August breeze blow in. With an open floor plan, the atmosphere was collaborative, allowing our twenty-plus team members to brainstorm together and chat openly throughout the day. It was the warm, inviting, creative space I'd imagined, but it was also an adjustment for me to be physically separated from the production process. It felt strange, and even a little sad, to be apart from the deodorant that I'd worked so intimately with from day one. Between the Florida offices, the co-packer on the East Coast, and our downtown Portland space, the teams were really spread out now. Even though it had been a gradual process of letting go and accepting that I couldn't possibly control all of the moving pieces of the company, it was still difficult. That process was made a little easier because of the fact that I had faith in our leadership, including Gabriella's oversight of the production process. With an increasing number of calls and meetings coming up concerning the future of the business, it was helpful for me to have the time and space.

As September approached, we prepared to launch Schmidt's soap. I loved our final formulations and couldn't wait to finally release them to customers. In preparation for the launch, Chris and I wrote answers to myriad anticipated customer support questions ("What can you tell me about the ingredients?" "What certifications does it have?" "What does it smell like?" "What does it feel like?") and developed educational blog posts. We had conducted customer surveys prior to launch to anticipate pain points for customers and plan for them. Chris and our customer support manager created and conducted trainings so both the Portland and Florida departments were well informed about the product and knew how to talk about it with customers.

When it came to press, we sent a ton of samples to editors and influencers in advance and planned strategic announcement articles, embargoed until launch. On social media, we created hype around new "mystery" products.

We invested heavily in digital marketing at launch, especially targeting existing customers, encouraging them to spread the word. Our messaging explained that customers had been asking us for more products, and how, with our soap, you could now smell like Schmidt's all over. We made sure to point out how different our soaps were from other brands with their unique natural exfoliants and innovative ingredients like turmeric and charcoal, which was just beginning to garner hype. We also emphasized how our palm oil was sustainably harvested and certified by the Roundtable on Sustainable Palm Oil.

We conducted polls about which scent people wanted to try the most, with cute storybook-style illustrations of the soap and deodorant together, which fans loved. (A deodorant pushing a bar of soap on a swing? Rick, you're a genius.) We'd then contact stores with screenshots of positive customer responses saying things like, "Look at this post with five thousand engagements—you need to get our new soap on your shelves!"

On the website, we offered discounted bundles of deodorant and soap to incentivize purchases, and included travel-size soap freebies in subscription orders to help deodorant fans get on board with the new products.

We saw a ton of enthusiasm from customers. Many already kept multiple Schmidt's scents in their rotation and were eager to add soap to their collection. While deodorant remained our top seller, this marked our first successful expansion into new product territory. On Facebook, I announced: "Friends, you can no longer tease me with 'Schmidt's for your pits.' Here we have Schmidt's for the whole body. Welcoming these new bar soaps to the family is a historic moment for the brand." I was proud!

"Do" diligence

When we received interest from two of the largest CPG companies in the world, it was exhilarating and mind-boggling. These large companies were known as "strategics," big companies that strategically make acquisitions—in consideration of their entire portfolio—in order to further their business goals. We embarked on a due diligence process with each. This meant providing a complete historical assessment of our company's finances, tax history, supply chain, marketing strategies, staff, IT structure, and so forth. A couple years prior, we'd hired an accountant to go back and correct the Schmidt's books from the early days when I didn't yet have a system in place. I'd turned over all my personal statements so business expenses and income could be parsed out. It was a messy, time-consuming job, but now it meant we could share information about finances as required. The diligence process included hundreds of questions and requests, such as:

- How large is your consumer database and how many data points are there per consumer?

- What are manufacturing cycle times, batch sizes, tank storage capacity, packaging lines speed, and equipment?

- List all countries into which the Company sells or provides products or services, along with the annual dollar levels of sales into each country.

- Provide detail of new innovations and associated revenue and profitability assumptions.

- Provide a summary of key contract terms with suppliers including start and end dates, fixed and variable costs, and renewal terms.

Just looking at it made my head hurt. Where to begin? We gathered information and created an endless number of spreadsheets and documents; it was like writing a whole book—a *series* of books—detailing every aspect of the company's inner workings.

I worked closely with Chris, who took the lead on assembling most of the information; his fast, efficient work style was perfect for this task. Gradually, he uploaded all of the diligence information to a "data room" where it was viewable to all parties.

Around the time we started seeing acquisition interest, we began working with a broker, Goldman Sachs, who served as the intermediary between us and the other parties and helped keep us on track with deadlines. Meanwhile, we continued conversations with interested venture capitalists (VCs). If a deal with one of the strategics fell through, we'd still need cash to support the business.

Are you prepared to answer to investors?

HERE'S WHAT MOST INVESTORS WILL BE LOOKING FOR

- Reliable, historical sales data plus forecasts with supporting inferences or assumptions in trend data
- Clarity on your personal wants/needs regarding a partnership or exit
- A thorough understanding of your target market and consumer demographics
- A comprehensive roadmap of your company's growth plan—new products, territories, and sales channels you intend to grow
- Data on every partnership, contract, retailer, and campaign in your company's history, along with customer data from your website (for example, most are on the West Coast, or the average purchase is twenty-five dollars)
- Everything that comes along with due diligence—make sure you have the data.

Meanwhile, Michael kept talking about another option: taking the company public. But, I didn't want to hire an investment bank to underwrite the process, and I believed that Schmidt's wasn't yet positioned to have a successful IPO (initial public offering). Taking on an IPO meant tougher regulatory requirements, and that we would need greater infrastructure to guarantee a successful listing—and at minimum, a fully built-out executive team and board. To me, the plan was grandiose and unrealistic, and I had no interest in pursuing it.

When there are moments to celebrate, take them

Over the summer, I'd received an invitation to go on a trade mission to Japan with the governor of Oregon, Kate Brown. Her delegation was traveling with select women business leaders. The trip would last about four days (plus travel) and included a "Doing Business in Oregon" seminar, a US Embassy briefing, and a women's leadership panel, among other events. I had barely ever traveled outside the country (aside from trips to Canada and Mexico), and the opportunity to go on a business trip to Japan took me completely by surprise. I wasn't sure I had the time in my schedule or that it made sense, but the more I considered it, the more appealing it seemed. It could be a good opportunity for Schmidt's, opening up a chance to expand to a new market. At the time, we didn't have any contacts in Japan, but when I asked, the delegation helped me set up meetings with two Japanese distributors. And frankly, I thought I could use a few days in a different environment. It was stressful for me to be away from my family and the office anytime I traveled, even to an expo or buyer meeting, but I always felt refreshed or newly inspired by the time I returned. Maybe a break across the world wouldn't be such a bad thing.

So in early October 2017, I flew to Tokyo along with Alison, a member of the Schmidt's marketing team, who accompanied me as my assistant to help with various tasks like managing my calendar. Right away I was struck by how clean the city was, not to mention enormous and modern. More importantly, I was energized by being completely out of my element. Our meetings were inspiring; I sat in on a briefing by the US Embassy staff, attended a Friends of Oregon Governor's reception, and had a "women's night out," where I mingled with local Japanese businesswomen, as well as those who'd traveled to the event. Participating in the women's leadership panel was the highlight of the journey. I sat alongside five women—four of them Japanese—to talk about the issues facing women in business today. The candid conversation was an inspiring shift in perspective for me. I was so absorbed in the daily demands of running my business that I didn't usually get to reflect on the complications, challenges, and rewards of being a woman business owner. The experience on the panel stayed with me and later helped shine a light on how I might play a more meaningful role in this broader conversation.

At one point, I asked my fellow panelists what we could all do to help make sure more companies fostered working conditions that empower women to be successful. Governor Brown's response resonated with me: "Many of us are mothers," she said. "We can make sure every young man we bring into the world recognizes the power and potential of women. Leading by example and impacting the next generation will make the difference." I thought of little Oliver back at home, now seven years old, who had grown up seeing me build Schmidt's. He was now old enough to have an understanding of what that meant. Recently, I'd been featured on the local news, and when we watched at home, his whole face lit up. "Is that really you?" he asked, grinning in disbelief. I treasured small moments like these, when Oli got a glimpse of my work world.

I was proud of how I'd balanced motherhood and running a business all these years. Since Oliver was born, I had ended nearly every day the same way: snuggled up with him in his bed, side by side, talking, singing, telling stories, laughing, and cuddling until he began to fall asleep. I'd always done everything I could to be present with him, to create routines and stability, to build memories, to show him all the love in the world. Still, there were plenty of times I felt guilty for not being home enough, bringing my work home with me, or being distracted by the stresses of the business. I had to remind myself that any working mom faces similar challenges; even if I wasn't leading Schmidt's, I'd still likely be working full time (and less fulfilled by the work). Now the opportunity to build a different kind of life was in reach, if we sold Schmidt's—a life where Chris and I would have much more time and flexibility, and our family would have financial security like we'd never known. I felt more and more ready to embrace it. It was time.

Shortly after I returned from my trip, in mid-October, Chris threw me a big fortieth birthday party. So many people showed up: my parents (who flew in from Michigan, along with my aunt and her partner), Ben, Alex, and many other Schmidt's employees, our tight-knit group of friends from the days of working together at the children's center, and other longtime friends. All of my favorite people were in one room together, at a nice venue near the river downtown, with catered food, special cocktails, music, and a photo booth. Looking around the room, I felt overcome by an enormous sense of gratitude for the people who had been by my side and supported me in their own special ways. It simultaneously felt like a lifetime ago and like no time had passed at all since I moved to Portland and started this new life. It was bewildering and amazing to think of all that had happened since then. Chris. Oliver. Schmidt's. Discovering a way to help manage my voice. I gave a short toast, thanking everyone profusely for being there, especially Chris, for being my partner in so many ways throughout it all. As a final surprise, he had made a slideshow of my life, narrated by Oliver's sweet voice, which was so beautiful and perfect, it left me in tears (and still does, every time I rewatch it). So much was changing and so much was still undetermined, but in that moment, I felt only the warm, loving presence of my friends and family, of being celebrated, and of having made it this far.

Take it over the finish line

In early November, we received disturbing news from Goldman Sachs: one of the two strategics interested in acquiring Schmidt's had pulled out. Evidently they'd chosen to "go another route." It was exactly what I'd feared: the whole deal could fall apart without warning. If that strategic could change course so abruptly, then Unilever, the other, might certainly do the same.

To make matters worse, we soon found out that one of our competitors had been acquired. We were aware of this particular competitor's increasing popularity and knew they were pitching to potential acquirers, but we didn't think they'd get picked up so soon. What did this mean for our potential deal? Would their valuation amount impact our own? Schmidt's had been around longer, had significant retail distribution, and for many other reasons, we viewed our company as more valuable. But a lower offer for them might result in a lower one for us, too. I hated to think about how the large company that had backed out knew so much about *our* strategies now, having sat through multiple presentations about our capabilities and received so much information through the diligence process. Even with NDAs signed, it felt unsettling. The entire situation was destabilizing, both personally and for the business.

Meanwhile, the possibility of the business running out of money was a real threat. Preparing for our Costco launch was an enormous investment. The big-box store required packaging unlike that of any other retailer, and for months we'd been designing special three-pack containers and an assortment of carefully designed display boxes. Since the outer packaging seal wouldn't allow shoppers to smell the deodorant, I'd been working to develop little perfume patches—like scratch-and-sniff stickers—to be included on each box. The money required to produce, package, and ship the deodorant was significant, not to mention the money needed for promo, advertising, and everything else we needed to make sure the launch was a success. Funds were significantly tied up in this launch and therefore running very low.

We had to stay focused on getting Unilever whatever they needed as the diligence process progressed. We continued to communicate with and provide information to a few venture capital firms, just in case the deal fell through, or an acquisition took so long that we needed an infusion of cash to continue operating before a deal was final. Everything was in a delicate balance. I was feeling anxious and unsettled, and was working my butt off, often late into the evening. Any sleep I was getting was interrupted when I would wake up in the middle of the night to write myself "don't forget to" notes.

Suddenly, another big strategic unexpectedly entered the mix, resulting in another diligence process and more meetings. Things had reached a fever pitch and we wanted to close a deal—soon. The week of Thanksgiving, Goldman Sachs helped us schedule an all-day meeting with Unilever on Monday, and another with the new strategic on Tuesday.

On Monday morning, Chris and I arrived for our first meeting, which had been arranged as a catered breakfast at a hotel in Portland (our own office was too small and lacked the privacy required). On the Schmidt's side, Chris, Michael, two members from our finance team, and I all took seats at the long conference table, across from about eight people from Unilever and four from Goldman Sachs. I was the first to speak. I'd strategically timed my vocal cord treatment in advance so that I'd feel confident using my voice as much as necessary. When I stood up in front of the group—most of them men in suits, many of whom had flown in from London just for this meeting—I felt overcome by a sense of assuredness and pride. In my everyday life, I wasn't the type to blather on about my achievements, but a meeting like this was not the time to hold back. I knew my story was special; I knew what I'd created was one of a kind. Unilever was beyond impressive, even intimidating, but I had something unique: I'd gotten here from the ground level, using just the raw materials, and I'd done it through passion and hard work. My product wasn't developed by experts in a lab. I *made* it. I told the story—my story—of spending those hours at my kitchen stove, applying to get into farmers markets, carrying Oliver on my hip into co-ops, taking a leap of faith by quitting my day jobs. Through years of hard work, I'd become the lead of a company with 150-plus employees with no slowdown in sight. I spoke with the same passion I'd had from the beginning, and the words flowed easily. I didn't feel like I had to sell anything or impress anybody; I only needed to share the truth. When I finished, I sat down, satisfied, with a huge smile on my face. I'd never heard myself speak as confidently and eloquently as I had during that meeting.

The rest of the meeting went smoothly. Chris delivered a powerful presentation on our marketing strategies and retail performance, as well as our view on how Schmidt's would fit within the Unilever family of products. I was impressed by Unilever's genuine interest in Schmidt's. They asked smart questions and listened sincerely. Most importantly, it was clear they wanted to own Schmidt's without compromising our values. They understood the value of our secret sauce and were eager to learn. Of course, by acquiring us, they wanted to get their hands on my recipe. But massive companies like Unilever have sophisticated labs and expert technicians, and they probably could have come close enough to replicating my formula on their own, if they'd really wanted to. What they couldn't replicate was the brand we'd built, with its loyal customer following—many of whom had been behind us since the very beginning. On top of that, our innovative marketing strategies had positioned Schmidt's as much more than a deodorant brand; we were a lifestyle, a movement, a force. That's not easy to create overnight, especially not for a global company that doesn't exude the kind of persona a small brand does.

It was obvious that Unilever could offer exceptional support and oversight as Schmidt's grew. I saw them as one of the biggest, most established, most progressive consumer packaged goods companies in the world, and their capabilities were impressive: extensive distribution channels, sophisticated consumer insights, a wealth of additional suppliers, their own in-house seasoned experts, and much more could be used to support and expand Schmidt's in a way that was in keeping with our values. Just the idea of Schmidt's becoming part of this strong, secure company with all of its expertise and connections put me at ease. We wouldn't have to face all that growth and expansion ahead of us on our own. An acquisition would have major benefits for both sides.

Following the big meeting, there were breakout sessions focused on specific topics like bookkeeping and human resources, then we all headed to our production space to give the team a tour. But first, I had scheduled time with Unilever to talk about my goals for the company and what I personally wanted for my role at Schmidt's if we agreed to move forward together with the acquisition.

Personally, I was debating whether I wanted to continue at an executive level or move to a position that was more removed from operations. Even though I was thrilled by the company's hypergrowth and excited to be doing more in product development with a roadmap of innovations ahead, being an executive at a large corporation didn't interest me as much as exploring new opportunities. Still, I wasn't willing to walk away from Schmidt's entirely—that was unimaginable to me. I wanted to continue to have a role at Schmidt's, especially as the brand expanded globally. What I really wanted was to be lifted of the burden of running the business and to have more time for Oliver and Chris and for other opportunities the future might hold for me. I was looking for a way to stay connected with the brand and help preserve its legacy, while gaining the freedom I'd been seeking.

We agreed that I would stay on as spokesperson for Schmidt's and transition away from the day-to-day operations. I felt secure in knowing that Unilever valued my best interests and would work with me to create a forward-looking position that would most benefit the brand.

When we met with a different company the following day, I didn't feel the same connection. Their capabilities were not as impressive as Unilever's, and I wasn't as confident that they "got" the brand. I was worried they might simply assimilate Schmidt's into their broader mechanisms, without attention to our values and key team members. Around this time, yet another huge company also showed interest, but it was clear to me that Unilever was the best fit. Goldman Sachs set a deadline for offers—December 8th, just two short weeks away—and we waited. When Unilever sent in an offer (one that exceeded all my expectations) on the deadline, my emotions were almost unbearable: a rush of excitement and relief. A few days later, I flew to New York City to work out the remaining details and (hopefully) sign the paperwork in person.

We all arrived at the office of Unilever's attorneys with the goal of finalizing all terms of the agreement. Goldman Sachs brokers were there, along with a swath of everyone's attorneys. We convened for discussions in a big conference room with a view of the New York City skyline, then used smaller breakout rooms to talk with our attorneys one on one about items we still needed to reach agreement on and reconvened in the big room. The sums, expectations, and benchmarks were still being negotiated. I had done so much up to this point to set Schmidt's up for success, including conceiving of and developing new products that weren't released yet, plus preparing us for expanded distribution in stores like Costco and CVS. If Schmidt's was successful in the future, I knew it would be in large part because of the groundwork I had laid, and so I actively negotiated for a deal that accounted for that accrued value.

Negotiations continued between our attorneys for hours. The clock was ticking, and we were on a deadline. Unilever requested the deal be signed by noon the following day, as they wanted to announce the acquisition at the holiday party at their New Jersey headquarters immediately afterwards. Chris was scheduled to fly in for the celebration, and I couldn't wait to see him once all was said and done.

Our terms remained unsettled into the evening, when Michael and I stepped away for a dinner reservation. He tended to be superstitious, and on our cab ride to the restaurant, he kept saying that if we were seated despite arriving late, it would be a good sign for the deal, whereas if we had missed our reservation, it would be a bad omen. I engaged in the joke with a nervous laugh.

Thankfully, when we arrived, despite being thirty minutes late for our reservation, we were seated. We ordered a bottle of champagne, then Michael spent much of the meal outside on his phone while I sat alone with my champagne, my thoughts all over the place.

We returned to the attorneys after dinner, around 11:00 P.M. After a few more hours of conversation—and still no settled agreement—Unilever requested follow-ups on a few diligence items, and I went back to the hotel to dig into the data on my laptop. We agreed to reconvene first thing in the morning—just a few hours away. Back at the hotel, I got into my pajamas and hopped into bed with my computer. I felt drained and delirious. Chris was en route but had gotten stuck on a layover in Detroit due to snow. He was currently trying to sleep in the lobby of an overbooked hotel, and we texted back and forth about our strange, dramatic evenings while I put together a few documents and emailed them. Finally, I closed my eyes. After ninety minutes of sleep I got right back out of bed, showered, and took a cab to the office at 7:00 A.M.

Time was ticking down. After a few more hours of back and forth, we had nearly come to terms. Shortly before our noon deadline, I excused myself and went to the bathroom. I was completely exhausted, overwhelmed, and feeling out of touch with my own emotions. (But more than anything, I had to pee.) In the bathroom, I glanced in the mirror, and it was as if I was looking at myself for the first time in years. I began to feel all the emotions—pride, confusion, excitement, fear, loss. I was minutes away from potentially saying goodbye to life as I'd known it for the past seven years. And despite being on the cusp of a thrilling, life-changing event, I knew that this change would also mean saying goodbye to a huge part of who I was, to the identity I'd arrived at with so much passion. I wanted to get back to myself, but at the same time, I didn't know who I would be without Schmidt's.

I said out loud, "Seems like I should cry or something." And as if on cue, the tears came.

I collected myself and returned to the boardroom, feeling liberated and ready to push this thing over the finish line. Just as I walked through the door, I watched as one of the key dealmakers threw his cell phone across the room, then stormed out, shouting something incoherent. *What was happening?*

I had no idea, but I knew I needed to be the one to fix it. I followed him down the hall, my heart racing. His face was crumpled in anger. "Hey," I said gently. "We're all tired, but we're gonna get through this. Let's take a minute to figure this out together." He took a deep breath and apologized. It turned out there was a simple misunderstanding about the paperwork. We were all at our wits' end, it seemed. Together, we walked back into the boardroom. It was just a few minutes before noon. The contract was sitting on the end of the table with a pen. At 11:59 A.M., I picked it up and signed.

Schmidt's had done it. Despite all of the challenges we'd faced, we overcame them, and everything we'd accomplished came together in this single, amazing moment. I took group photos with everyone in the boardroom, then jumped in a taxi to head to Unilever HQ for the big party.

Unilever's team had a press release about the acquisition scheduled for noon, so Chris and I had constructed a plan to let our employees know of the acquisition as quickly as possible. The team received real-time updates on any published news about Schmidt's, and if we didn't act fast, they'd hear about it before we reached them. (For various legal reasons, we weren't able to reveal the news until after we signed the deal.)

While I was in my taxi headed to the Unilever party, Chris arranged a conference call from his hotel in Detroit with us and the downtown Portland office, the Portland manufacturing warehouse, and the Florida offices. It was not the easiest call to make. I wished I could look my employees in the eyes and let them know what a great thing this was, and that everything was going to be okay. I'd always tried to be transparent, and I was very close with many of my colleagues, but throughout the diligence process, I'd had to keep my mouth shut about everything that was transpiring. Now I was making this big announcement from across the country, which I knew would feel unexpected and confusing for many of them, though there had been some buzz around the office about a potential investment. For a moment, the line was quiet after we revealed the news. Those were three of the longest seconds of my life, but then thankfully some members of the marketing team broke the silence with some celebratory hollers of congratulations. We explained that we understood how many questions and emotions this would generate amongst the team members, and Chris immediately followed up by speaking with each manager privately to review a game plan we'd prepared for communicating further, and for making plans for announcing the Unilever partnership to customers and media. I'm really not sure what kind of response I was expecting, but I was relieved the secret was no longer a secret.

When we pulled up to Unilever's headquarters, we were greeted at the door with blasting music, glasses of wine, a series of applause, and a whirlwind of introductions. The acquisition was announced in front of hundreds of employees, and I was pulled onstage and Schmidt's was welcomed as the newest member of the Unilever family. *How did I get here?* I thought. I was also fresh off a voice treatment, so my voice was softer than usual, making it difficult to speak up in a crowded room. Despite feeling completely overwhelmed (not to mention exhausted) I was buoyed by the Unilever employees' enthusiasm. Everybody was incredibly friendly and excited about having Schmidt's become part of the family.

We were invited to join an after-party at a nearby restaurant. Chris had finally caught a flight and was scheduled to land in time to meet us there. Before heading over, I took a quick moment for myself to sit down, exhausted, and exhale. I was so ready for Chris to be there and to anchor me back to normal—though what was normal now?

How to share big business news

HERE'S WHAT I SUGGEST PREPARING FOR IN THE IMMEDIATE TERM

Team communications. Anticipate many questions from the team. Be ready to have a candid and encouraging talk to clarify what this will mean for the business.

Customer support. Put together written responses to anticipated customer inquiries and a social media plan to support it.

Media/press. Create a press release and schedule interviews to support the news once it goes live.

When Chris arrived, a wave of comfort washed over me, and I ran over to embrace him. As the after-party wound down, we stepped out, and finally, it was just the two of us.

We wanted to find a place to get a drink and celebrate, but first, we headed back to the hotel so Chris could continue to coordinate with the marketing and customer support teams who would be responsible for responding to social media commentary as the news broke. I opened my computer to see there was plenty of buzz online already, not all of it positive. Some customers and fans said we were "selling out," which was painful to see. Most aggravating to me were comments from competitors who were capitalizing on the opportunity to capture our customers' attention. "We're still independent," one wrote. "Come on over to us!"

I closed my laptop. I understood the pushback, but it was a lot to take in. I knew the acquisition was what was best for Schmidt's, for my family, and for me. My philosophy from the beginning had been to make my product accessible, available to as many people as possible. The acquisition supported that vision, strengthened it, and made it possible for it to reach even further. I felt secure in knowing I had given Schmidt's my whole self.

Chris and I finally emerged from the hotel, leaving the noise behind. We wandered into a pub in Times Square, ordered Philly cheesesteaks and gin and tonics from the well, and basked in our newfound sense of freedom. The sum of money from the acquisition was beyond our wildest dreams and we were giddy with possibilities. We could buy our dream home, plan family vacations, and potentially start another business. I was forty years old—so much was ahead of me—and I felt at peace, optimistic Schmidt's was in good hands with Unilever. ∎

What to make of it

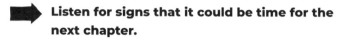 **Listen for signs that it could be time for the next chapter.**

For me, those signs were the need for capital investment as well as executive-level talent. Plus, I was daydreaming a lot about my next life phase. Both the business and I were ready.

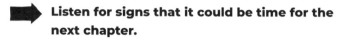 **The best opportunity for your company might be outside its four walls.**

When I started Schmidt's, I never dreamed I'd sell it. But by the time the opportunity arose, it was obvious it was the best thing for the company and for me. I knew I didn't want to go it alone any longer; I knew Schmidt's would find a good home with Unilever; I knew it was time. For many founders, an opportunity like this is a dream come true, while for others, the idea might take some warming up to. For me it was a little bit of both.

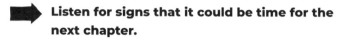 **Control your own story.**

In the late days of Schmidt's, the business had become too big to manage every aspect of it. I had to remember to take one day at a time, keep all things in perspective, and recognize how hard I had worked to get where I was. This was still my story, and I needed to make decisions that were best for me and my family. I knew selling the business might result in some backlash, but I had to trust I was making the best decision.

CHAPTER 12

Have greater impact.

Continue your mission and help level the playing field.

O n our first day back in Portland, Chris and I drove to work together as usual. I was nervous about facing everyone at the office. What did they really think about the news? I worried my employees, who had been so loyal to me, would feel they'd been left out of the loop and caught off guard.

We stood outside for a moment before going in. My heart thumped in my chest. As soon as I walked through the office door however, my nerves instantly faded away. Everyone cheered and was genuinely happy to see us. "Congratulations!" a few said, and I quickly realized just how eager I was to fill them in on everything that had happened. Chris and I sat in the middle of the office and told the story, with everyone gathered around. I found such comfort in sharing some of the details of how it all went down, and I emphasized how grateful I was for all the hard work the team had done to get us to this point. I said I wanted each of them to feel like this was their accomplishment, too. It really was. We'd gotten here together.

Naturally, there were a lot of questions about the transition. Some wanted to know if their jobs would change or if they'd get to visit the Unilever offices, as well as other logistics about how they'd be impacted.

The hardest part was explaining that I would no longer be leading the daily operations of the company. My agreement included a broad list of obligations, like being a face for the brand, supporting international expansion efforts, and offering insights into product development. But I wasn't sure how regular of a presence I should plan to have in the office moving forward. Everything I'd been doing for Schmidt's—product development, sales, approvals on marketing campaigns, operations oversight—was technically no longer my responsibility, and it was my job for the next few months to help transition those duties to other team members. It felt strange, all of a sudden, as I began to fully absorb the fact that I would no longer be managing the ins and outs of this company that had become such a part of me.

One thing that helped ease the transition was that Chris was staying on full time. In our negotiation process with Unilever, he'd chosen to continue overseeing the marketing department for six months before transitioning into a consultant role.

It was nearly Christmas, and Chris, Oliver, and I spent the holiday at home, trying to process everything and unwind. Oliver had participated so much in Schmidt's over the years, in his own way, like when he stayed up late with his nonna (Chris's mom) the night of the Entrepreneur of the Year Award, eagerly awaiting the results, or when he got excited about a new product we were launching, or whenever we spotted Schmidt's in a store. This was a transitional time for all of us and I wondered how he would feel about the news, if he would feel some kind of loss. I was relieved and happy when he seemed to embrace the change and seemed especially excited to hear that I would have much more time to spend at home with him.

It was nice to have some peace and quiet, but I was also anxiously awaiting confirmation that the deal had been officially finalized. There's a process where the government must approve an acquisition, which generally takes a couple weeks, and I couldn't help but feel unsettled without knowing it was completely locked in. Despite this, I chose to assume the best and celebrate the New Year's holiday with a family trip to San Diego, California, as the odds of something falling through at this point were slim. While we were there, on December 31, 2017, we got word that everything had been approved. It was done. I was overcome with emotion, the most obvious one being an enormous sense of relief. On New Year's Day morning, Chris, Oliver, and I took a breakfast cruise on the bay. It was a beautiful, mild day, and for a few hours we floated along, enjoying the buffet, the scenery, and each other. There's a photo of me on the boat, the sunshine on my face, grinning from ear to ear. I felt like I had a whole new life of possibilities ahead of me.

Jump into the next chapter

After the New Year's holiday, we returned to Portland, and on his first day back to work, Chris took Oliver to the bus stop on his way to the office—the way we used to do together—and then drove downtown. I was home alone, in a quiet, empty house. It felt amazing. I didn't realize how much I'd missed peacefulness and solitude until I had it back. I did our laundry and went to the grocery store in the middle of the day, when hardly anybody was there, and it felt like the biggest luxury. I wanted to exercise again, read books, cook, and greet Oli as he got off the bus after school. I was liberated.

But it was still deeply satisfying to have a hand in Schmidt's. In January, I worked with the Schmidt's team to help develop a scent in collaboration with Jane Goodall. The effort had been in progress before the acquisition, and I was excited to see it through. Goodall sent a list of proposed scents, and I identified two as my favorites: honeysuckle and lily of the valley. I ordered samples from one of our perfume houses and, when they arrived, went to the office to smell the variations. One version of lily of the valley was just perfect; the team all loved it, too. That fall, the collaboration was announced, with a percentage of proceeds from Lily of the Valley purchases going to the Jane Goodall Institute. Fast-forward eighteen months, when Schmidt's announced another celebrity partnership, this time with the one and only Justin Bieber. This is another project that had been discussed before the Unilever acquisition, and it was exciting to see it finally come to life. It's pretty mind-blowing that a big name like Justin Bieber appeared in a Schmidt's campaign.

That February, I spoke about my story of founding and growing the brand at Beautycon, where I was grateful to also spend some time hanging out at the Schmidt's booth with former colleagues, talking about the products. In March, Chris and I attended Natural Products Expo West, where we again enjoyed spending time at the booth, walking the floor, and exploring all of the other unique brands and products.

I'd also spend a few hours each day helping out with the Schmidt's emails still hitting my inbox. I had long-standing relationships with so many retailers, buyers, vendors, suppliers, and brokers, and I felt responsible for making sure their transition with Unilever went smoothly. I helped with whatever I could, but it was also refreshing to be able to type, "I'm no longer working in ops for Schmidt's, but I'm cc'ing so-and-so who can help you."

Every so often, I'd open a tab on my browser and log into my checking account. The moment our deal had gone through, the money from the sale was immediately transferred to me. When I first saw the number in *my* account, it felt completely surreal. I kept checking it, thinking it might disappear. I logged in, looked, logged out, and then would log in again a couple hours later. Was this real? It was hard to believe. I had to figure out what to do with it. It wasn't wise to leave the full amount sitting there. When news of the acquisition broke, a bunch of private investment bankers had reached out to Chris and me, eager to help us manage the money. We did our research, and in the weeks following the acquisition, talked with a dozen potential advisors. Of those, we narrowed it down to four we were impressed with (or more like less skeptical of), each of whom flew out to Portland to meet with us. When at last we chose one, I was comforted in having the support and guidance we needed to plan for our future.

At first, we had no formal plan. I can't overstate how strange it was that everything had actually happened. It took over a year after the acquisition to fully process everything and think about all the ways we could put our success to good use.

One of the first things we did in the spring of 2018 was search for a new house. We wanted to stay in Portland and find a place that was comfortable for our family, and especially for Oliver, with plenty of open space to play with friends, and a big yard outside to run around in. When we first walked into the house that would eventually become ours, Chris and I knew right away it was perfect. The neighborhood reminded me of Michigan, with towering trees like the ones in the Deep Dark Woods where I spent my days collecting acorns. On our next visit, we brought Oliver (who had final say on the matter), and he immediately fell in love too. In May, we moved in.

In June, Chris officially said goodbye to day-to-day work at Schmidt's, although he stayed involved as an innovation consultant for several months. Sometimes he and I scrutinized decisions the brand made, wondering if we would have done the same if it had been up to us, and we'd banter back and forth like two colleagues letting off steam at happy hour. But, generally we understood that the company's needs were changing quickly, and trusted the team we had put in place to steward the brand into its next chapter. At the time of writing this, I continue to work with Schmidt's, supporting global market launches, participating in press tours and events, and filming commercials as spokesperson.

Reconnect with community

In my farmers market days and in the early years of growing the business, community was everything. The first retailers who stocked Schmidt's helped me learn about pricing. Fellow makers inspired me at markets. My own network of friends and family supported me in myriad ways, like my friend Jeni, who would lend me her nose when I needed a second opinion, or Chris's mom, who helped label jars. Being surrounded by this community of peers and supporters was essential. But once Schmidt's really started to experience substantial growth, any time I might have had to nurture my community relationships was in low supply. For years I lived and breathed Schmidt's, with very little capacity to do much else, aside from spend time with my family. Now that I finally could, I was excited to re-immerse myself in this community.

With the extra time afforded by the acquisition, Chris, Oli, and I were able to spend more of our weekends at local craft fairs and street festivals, and when we vacationed out of town, we prioritized going to events and shops supporting local goods. It really stood out to me how much the community had evolved in the years since I had a booth of my own. On all those Sunday mornings, often the only other personal care competitor was a soap maker or two. Now there were entrepreneurs with facial serums, toners and tonics, organic makeup, and so much more—and they all had beautiful packaging, branding, and websites. The same was true with packaged foods and all kinds of other wares. These makers were intent on growing a business, not just exploring a hobby. But the scene had become so competitive, leaving me to wonder about the obstacles they were facing in moving their passion to the next level. How could I use my own expertise—accumulated through my years of tribulations and triumphs with Schmidt's—to help?

In the wake of the acquisition, entrepreneurs had been emailing me *nonstop*. I'd never experienced anything like it. It seemed that once news of the Unilever acquisition hit, my success caught the attention of business owners in a new way. People wanted to meet for coffee to "pick my brain," talk about their own business plans, and get my advice. "I've been building my own company for four years now and would love the opportunity to meet you for coffee or lunch sometime to learn more about your path and experience in entrepreneurship, especially in moving to the next level of national distribution," read one message. Another wanted to connect me with a colleague to discuss "how to think about talking to investors and strategic buyers." Another described being at a business crossroads and hoped to "set up a meeting to see if you might be able to steer us in the right direction." "I really admired the work you did with Schmidt's Naturals and was wondering if you do any private consultation for independent businesses who wish to grow (*cough* like mine)," wrote another.

There *was* so much I wanted to say and offer, but there was no way I could sit down for one-on-ones with every single person who emailed me. I started to wonder if maybe I could open myself up for "office hours" once a month at a venue where at least the local small business owners and makers could stop by and chat with me. Or maybe I could even do it by conference call so that I could connect with those outside of Portland. I entertained a few of these options, but nothing felt like the right solution. When the idea of writing a book came up, it seemed like the perfect opportunity: I could offer insights and lessons from my own entrepreneurial journey in a way that would reach the largest group of people. True to form, Chris became my biggest supporter, urging me to get writing.

That summer, Jim from Portland Made—a local collective of entrepreneurs and makers that hosts educational gatherings for networking and business development—reached out and invited me to stop by an upcoming event. "You're a maker rock star and very much looked up to in our community. It would mean a lot to have you there. Come on by?" he wrote. I'd known about Portland Made for years but never had a chance to attend an event. With more time on my hands, I was eager to check it out. Chris and I spent the evening mingling with makers and small business owners, chatting over snacks and cocktails and exchanging business cards. Soon afterwards, Jim invited me to speak at a Portland Made meetup on the theme of "Scaling Schmidt's Naturals." It was held inside a local printmaker's studio. Of course, I'd had experience speaking at award ceremonies, conferences, and business events, but something about speaking to this smaller audience of passionate entrepreneurs—*my* people—inspired me in a whole different way.

Expand your purpose

In the months after the acquisition, Chris and I formed our own investment fund, named Color, which we operate as the sole owners. Recognizing the instutional barriers to funding, we made it our goal through Color to invest in a more equitable system by supporting and investing in underrepresented founders. We understood, too, the added value we could bring to these businesses with the wealth of knowledge we'd gained from growing Schmidt's to an acquisition. We wanted to make the founder-investor relationship more accessible, down to earth, and easier to navigate, while helping brands grow their bottom lines through strategic growth marketing, retail expansion, and creative storytelling.

At the time of writing, Color has made about a dozen investments, and we are approached daily by companies interested in what we are bringing to the table. As we become known for our thesis-driven approach and unique skillsets as investors, I believe our impact will only grow, serving to facilitate the goals of like-minded founders in the pursuit of inclusivity and a redefined future for consumer products.

Chris and I were in constant conversation about how we might be able to support others, beyond Color's funding capabilities. From the moment we'd met at our jobs at the treatment center for children, we had been working together side by side—we were ready for this exciting next adventure.

We began conceptualizing the launch of Supermaker: an inclusive media platform that elevated emerging entrepreneurs and promoted modern workplace thinking. We wanted to be a voice for those often excluded from traditional media outlets, primarily women and people of color. We saw an opportunity to create a platform where we could curate answers to the kinds of entrepreneurial questions I was being asked, and much more. We wanted to celebrate entrepreneurs and the creative community with artful storytelling, resources, and events, alongside articles with a conscious, progressive agenda.

I'd learned through my own journey just how game-changing it was to get wider notice and attention. What if we could help shine a light on founders and brands *before* they got on the radar of traditional media outlets? Or tell the stories of more established brands in a different way? And what if we could facilitate important conversations about workplace inclusivity and social responsibility? What if we could host our own events to emphasize our efforts on the ground? As the months rolled on, we kept visualizing and honing our idea.

It was a way not only to change the narrative for aspiring and early stage entrepreneurs, but also to merge everything we'd learned, from general business management and best practices, to branding, marketing, and PR, to taking on investment or following through with an acquisition. We began collaborating with artists and founders from across the globe to bring it to life. More than anything, we grew excited about the power of media and the importance of shining a light on underrepresented voices in times like these. Just like we had been driven to "change the way you think about deodorant," we were now set to change the way people thought about business media.

In June 2019, while deep in the process of writing my *Supermaker* book, we launched the Supermaker platform. At the time of writing, we're also working towards rolling out Supermaker Radio, a podcast series to complement the book, and a Supermaker grant program called "Playing Field," which awards female and nonbinary founders grants to help grow their businesses.

Finding my voice

In the spring of 2019, I flew to Europe to join the Unilever team for the official Schmidt's launch in the EU. While the brand had been available in the EU for years (think back to that first Netherlands order I mailed myself in 2013), now Unilever was rolling out a more extensive, official launch to the European market. I spent a week in Amsterdam, London, and Paris, giving back-to-back presentations to media, attending press events, and meeting with key retailers. In Rotterdam, I took the stage at Unilever's headquarters and told my founding story to the global brand teams, which would be valuable for their understanding and for pitching the brand in their regions. A few months later, I engaged in a similar press tour in Toronto. I look forward to more opportunities to play a part in the global expansion of Schmidt's, as the brand grows across Europe and into other markets like Australia, Brazil, and Southeast Asia.

I'd come a long way since that moment on stage at Fox News. After the Unilever partnership (and thanks to my vocal treatments and the dozens of speaking engagements under my belt), I felt more secure than ever in my public speaking. Plus, I no longer felt like I had to convince anyone of anything in a sales-y way; instead, I could simply tell my story. Today, one of my greatest passions is appearing on podcasts, television, and radio, or standing in front of a roomful of engaged listeners.

Meanwhile, Chris and I were still in conversation with Jim of Portland Made, who had news for us: he said he might be taking on a new job and selling the organization. We discussed possibilities, and Chris and I made the decision to acquire it. We believed in Portland Made's positive impact and knew we could help ensure its longevity, expanding on its offerings without disrupting what already made it special. It's been the perfect complement to all we are doing with Color and Supermaker, but rooting us on the ground in Portland.

Initially, I imagined my next chapter in life consisting of slow, quiet days. That changed when I was reintroduced to the makers who had that same determination within them, and it was easy to see a new story for myself. Having so recently experienced the searching and the self-doubt, the disappointments and the discovery, the risks and the hope, the plunges and the climb to victories small and large, I wanted to take the lessons of my past and offer them to those coming up behind me. My hope is that you'll find just that in the pages of this book.

One of the most meaningful parts of writing has been recalling my own early journey of self-discovery—trying all kinds of jobs (hot dog chef included), moving to a new city, taking classes, involving myself in the community, and absorbing inspiration from the creatives and friends who surrounded me. I allowed myself to experiment, find value in all kinds of experiences, and change direction multiple times. And it's only through that earnest, relentless pursuit that I was able to discover my purpose. In a sense, I'm in a similar position now. My new endeavors and second half of life are just beginning to take shape, and I'm not sure yet where the path will lead. What I learned by growing Schmidt's is that I'm more resilient than I ever realized. I have no plans to stop getting my hands dirty, saying yes, or confronting setbacks head on.

My wish for makers and entrepreneurs today is that you allow yourselves this same sense of freedom and adventure in your own endeavors. Be open. Don't settle. Pay attention to what lights you up, and follow it. Be willing to change course. Surround yourself with a proper support system, and support others in return. Trust your intuition, and always stand by your values. These are the guiding principles that carry me forward, and I hope they inspire you, too. Together as Supermakers, there's no limit to what we can achieve. ∎

Acknowledgments

I would like to acknowledge and thank the special people who contributed to my entrepreneurial success and helped make this book possible:

First, my husband, Chris, who encouraged me to share my story with the world. For always doing everything in his strength to support and elevate me. For his marketing mastery, brilliant mind, and diehard devotion. For his work with the art direction and editing of this book.

My son, Oliver, who was the real inspiration behind exploring my passion and starting my business. For offering candid insights and being a patient participant in countless conversations about work. For all of our shared nighttime cuddles and Garfield episodes that helped keep me grounded.

My parents, John and Pam, and my brother, Jason, for giving me all the love and comforts I could ask for growing up. For straightening the deodorant shelves at their local retailers and convincing strangers in the aisles to buy Schmidt's.

My mother-in-law, Pam, who has always been generous with her love and support, helping out on a whim with babysitting Oliver or putting in extra hours at Schmidt's when I was overloaded.

All the employees and partners who have ever worked for Schmidt's, for jumping in with enthusiasm, powering through challenges, and sharing in victories. For learning with me along the way and helping me grow into a leader.

The customers who took a chance on me at the farmers markets, who shared their feedback with me, and who remained loyal to the Schmidt's brand over the years. Also, the retailers who made space on their shelves and believed in what I was doing.

Chronicle Books; Janklow & Nesbit, notably Emma Parry; and Unfurl Productions, who made writing and publishing this book a reality. And the individuals who helped me articulate my most authentic story: Cara Bedick, Kelly Shetron, and Natalie Byrne. Also talented illustrator and friend Rick DeLucco.

My cherished friends, old and new, who have all offered love and support in their own special ways.

About the Author

Jaime Schmidt is an entrepreneur and the founder of Schmidt's, a global leader in natural personal care products, which she started from her kitchen in Portland, Oregon, in 2010. Jaime is credited with leading a movement to modernize the naturals industry and increase its accessibility to the mainstream. Under her leadership, Schmidt's grew into a household name, lining the shelves of retailers, including Target, Costco, Whole Foods, Walmart, and CVS, across more than thirty countries. In 2017, Schmidt's was acquired by global consumer goods company Unilever.

Today, Jaime is focusing her efforts on helping emerging entrepreneurs pursue their own dreams. In June 2019, she launched Supermaker, a media platform celebrating diverse, independent brands and modern workplace values.

Additionally, Jaime is the co-founder of Color, an inclusive investment fund that finances and supports the growth of consumer-facing companies.

She is regularly profiled in prominent business media including *Inc.*, *Entrepreneur*, *Forbes*, and *Fast Company*.

Jaime is an inaugural member of the Inc. Founders Project, and has also been recognized as one of the 100 Most Intriguing Entrepreneurs (Goldman Sachs, 2017 and 2018), PNW Entrepreneur of the Year (Ernst & Young, 2017), one of *Inc.*'s Female Founders 100, and one of the Create & Cultivate 100.

Jaime currently resides in Portland, Oregon, with her husband and business partner, Chris Cantino; their son, Oliver; and KK, their munchkin cat.

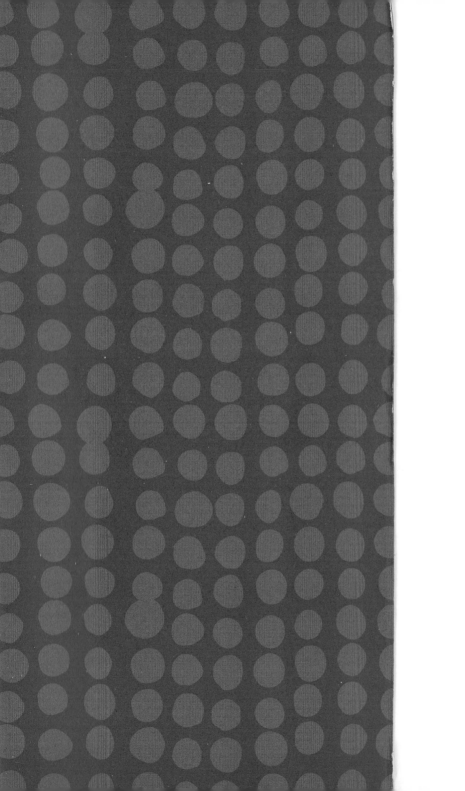

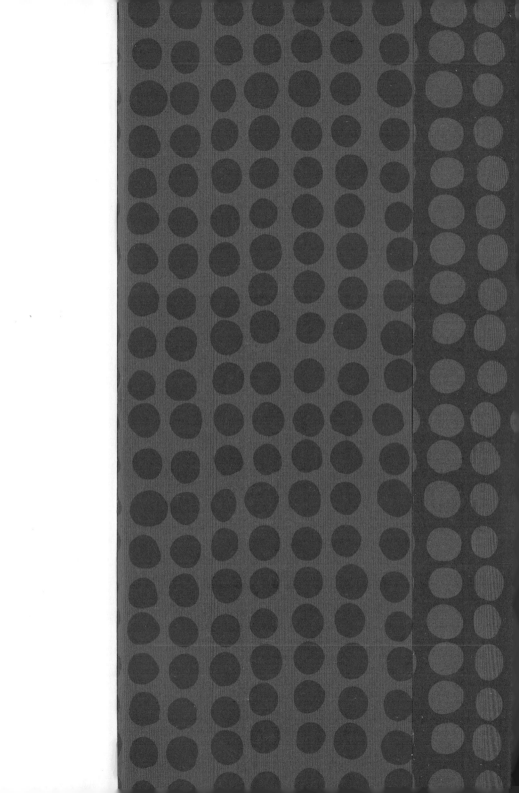